A PRACTICAL STEP BY STEP GUIDE

HANGING BASKETS
AND WALL CONTAINERS

A PRACTICAL STEP BY STEP GUIDE

HANGING BASKETS

AND WALL CONTAINERS

JENNY HENDY
WITH PHOTOGRAPHS BY NEIL SUTHERLAND

Trafalgar Square Publishing

First published in the United States of America in 2002
by Trafalgar Square Publishing, North Pomfret, Vermont 05053

Some of the material that appears in this book was previously published
in *A Creative Step-by-step Guide to Hanging Baskets and Wall
Containers*, also by Jenny Hendy.

ISBN 1 57076 210 4

Library of Congress Card Catalog Number: 2001092646

Credits

Designed and edited by: FOCUS PUBLISHING,
The Courtyard, 26 London Road,
Sevenoaks, Kent TN13 1AP
Designers: Sam Hemphill, Philip Clucas
Editors: Guy Croton, Caroline Watson
Photographer: Neil Sutherland
Illustrator: Tim Heyward, courtesy of Bernard Thornton Artists
Editorial director: Will Steeds

THE AUTHOR

Jenny Hendy has always been excited by plants and gardening and
by the time she started school was already entering horticultural
competitions! A freelance writer for the last ten years, she has written
and contributed to many titles. She now divides her time between
books and magazines and running her own garden design consultancy.

THE PHOTOGRAPHER

Neil Sutherland has more than 25 years' experience in a wide range
of photographic fields, including still-life, portraiture, reportage, natural
history, cookery, landscape, and travel. His work has been published in
countless books and magazines throughout the world.

CONTENTS

INTRODUCTION

Making the Most of Hanging Baskets 10–11

THE BASICS

Types of Hanging Basket 14–15
Liners and Composts 16–17
Preparing Your Basket 18–19
Choosing Your Plants 20–25
Color Guide 26–31
Establishing Your Basket 32–33
Where and How to Hang Your Basket 34–35
Feeding and Watering 36–37
Vacation Care for Hanging Baskets 38–39
A Backdrop for the Basket 40–41
Making an Impact with Baskets 42–43

THE PROJECTS

A Self-Watering Spring Basket 46–47
Hyacinths and Primulas 48–49
Buckets Full of Bulbs 50–51
A Spring Wall Basket 52–53
Silver Baskets of Campanulas 54–55
Fragrant Jasmine in a Black Wire Basket 56–57
A Cottage Garden Basket 58–59
Painting Pots for a Weathered Look 60–61
A Character Wall Pot with Ivy Hair 62–63
Planting Up for Summer 64–65
A Shallow Basket 66–67
Red Geraniums in an Elegant
   Wirework Basket 68–69
A Summer Basket with a Purple Theme 70–71

Hostas in a Woodland Basket
   for a Shady Place 72–73
A Pink Basket for Cool Shade 74–75
Thyme, Sage, and Verbena 76–77
A Summer Display in a Manger Basket 78–79
A Classic White Arrangement 80–81
A Romantic Wall Basket 82–83
A Wall Basket of Portulucas
   for a Hot Sunny Spot 84–85
Grass and Succulents in a
   Terracotta Wall Pot 86–87
A Cascade of White and Gold 88–89
A Large Display of Purple and Yellow 90–91
A Subtropical Hanging Basket 92–93
A Late-Season Pastel Display 94–95
Dahlias in a Wicker Basket 96–97
Violas and Ivy with a Fuchsia for Foliage 98–99
An Ivy Chicken Basket 100–101
A Large Winter Display 102–103
A Cheerful Basket of Evergreens 104–105
Eye-Catching Pots of Gold 106–107
A Winter Wall Basket with Berries 108–109
A Basket of Pansies 110–111
Ferns in an Oriental Basket 112–113

PLANT IDENTIFIER

A–Z of Hanging Basket Plants 128–137

Index 138–139
Acknowledgments 140–141

MAKING THE MOST OF HANGING BASKETS

Hanging baskets and wall pots allow you to cultivate what is to all intents and purposes a hostile environment—the wall of a house is like a sheer cliff face with no toeholds! But fix in a few screws, hooks, and brackets and you can transform bare bricks into luxuriant hanging gardens.

HANGING BASKET BENEFITS

The wonderful thing about baskets is that the display is only temporary. You can ring the changes from year to year and from season to season and have great fun experimenting with different plants and color schemes. Go ahead and break some gardening rules! Mix alpines with bedding plants, houseplants with herbs, and shrubs with tender perennials—you will be surprised at how good the results can be. Once you branch out into using plants other than those traditionally associated with baskets, the palette of colors and textures available increases enormously. Baskets and wall pots are available in a wide range of materials and designs, some more practical than others. On the following pages you will find detailed and comprehensive advice on all practical aspects of hanging basketmaking, both indoors and outside.

BASKETS AS FEATURES

There is no need to keep buying new baskets. As this book shows, you can recycle the same container through the seasons, using a variety of colors and plant associations to produce strikingly different results each time. Generally speaking, hanging baskets are a feature of the summer garden, but this certainly does not have to be the case. This book takes you through the seasons, with ideas on what plants are available at the time and where to find them in the garden center. Even in the depths of winter, you can enjoy wonderful displays of fresh flowers, colorful berries, and foliage around the door of your home.

This book will teach you how to create superb hanging displays matching the colors and form of flowers and foliage to the walls of your house or any other backdrop you choose for your basket. It will help you creatively enhance your home.

Hanging baskets are a versatile and attractive planting medium. A flower pouch like this enables spectacular displays.

A superb hanging basket packed to the brim with an extensive selection of spring flowers and bulbs. Not all arrangements need be so sumptuous in order to be effective.

THE BASICS

Types of Hanging Basket **14**

Liners and Composts **16**

Preparing Your Basket **18**

Choosing Your Plants **20**

Color Guide **26**

Establishing Your Basket **32**

Where and How to Hang Your Basket **34**

Feeding and Watering **36**

Maintaining Your Basket While You Are Away **38**

A Backdrop for the Basket **40**

Making an Impact with Baskets **42**

TYPES OF HANGING BASKET

Nowadays there is a phenomenal selection of plant containers to choose from. The types of hanging basket and wall container available are almost as numerous as those which stand on the ground, and if you really cannot make your mind up or want something truly unique, you could always make your own.

WIRE HANGING BASKETS

Traditionally lined with sphagnum moss, but other liners may be used. The wire is usually coated with black, green, or white plastic. This kind of basket tends to dry out more quickly, so pick the larger sizes with a greater soil volume, for example 14in or 16in diameter. Baskets with a large mesh size allow for planting through the sides.

Above: *Plastic baskets come in many different designs and colors and are easy to work with, relatively inexpensive, and widely available.*

SELF-WATERING BASKETS

If you can't water regularly, this kind of basket is ideal. Designs vary, but each has a reservoir with a wick that allows the compost to draw water up from below as required. Some also have an overflow device.

PLASTIC HANGING BASKETS

These come with chains or plastic snap-on hangers and often feature a detachable drip tray. They tend not to dry out as quickly as traditional wire baskets and are available in a range of colors.

WICKER HANGING BASKETS

You don't see these around too often, but the woven wicker finish is ideal for a more rustic or cottage garden setting. They are sometimes pre-lined with plastic but, if not, cut plastic sheeting to fit so that the wicker is kept dry.

WALL BASKETS

These may be ceramic or terracotta, often with a classical or romantic design. You can also get simple plastic wall planters. More

Wire baskets lined with sphagnum moss are widely used as versatile hanging containers. They are easy to plant up and will hang anywhere—perhaps from an ornate bracket, as in this case—but they do tend to dry out quickly and require frequent watering.

Above: Wall baskets come in all shapes and sizes in many different materials.

Above: Flower towers and wall pots combine well to make abundant and varied displays. Both are particularly useful for disguising plain exterior walls or unattractive backyards.

like traditional wire hanging baskets, wire mesh wall baskets allow planting through the sides. Manger baskets and hay racks, usually made from black-painted wrought iron or heavy-duty plastic-coated wire, come in a variety of shapes and sizes, the larger ones being suitable for semi-permanent displays.

NOVELTY BASKETS

You can make hanging baskets out of all kinds of containers, simply by attaching some kind of hanging device. Butcher's hooks or "S" hooks are useful for hanging up baskets, metal buckets and other containers that already have handles.

FLOWER TOWERS/ HANGING POCKETS

Flower towers consist of a plastic tube with a rigid ring at the top to which the hanging chains are attached and have a drip tray at the bottom. This is filled with compost and the sides slit with a sharp knife to allow for

planting. Single plantings look best, giving the effect of a hanging column of flowers. Plastic hanging pockets are hung on the wall and the pockets planted up with trailers.

Above: You can make your own novelty containers and baskets from just about anything that will hold a plant. Here a collection of old boots and shoes has been put to good use.

15

LINERS AND COMPOSTS

Liners and composts provide the environment in which the plants that you select for your hanging baskets and wall containers must live, so they should always be chosen with care. With liners, there is also an aesthetic consideration to bear in mind: if the liner is visible once the basket is planted up, will it be attractive, or an eyesore?

LINERS FOR WIRE BASKETS

Sphagnum moss Attractive when fresh and green, it gives a newly planted basket a more established look. With regular watering the soft, moist texture protects the delicate shoots and roots of cuttings planted through the basket sides. Used as a thick surface mulch, it seals in moisture and prevents soil erosion when watering. Moss goes brown if allowed to dry out or is kept in the dark, and you may unwittingly buy brown moss in sealed opaque bags.

Above: Manufactured liners now come in a wide variety of materials and designs.

Conifer clippings When they are cut for winter baskets, these will remain green for months. For a 14-inch basket, cut soft shoot tips around 8 or 9 inches long from a hedge and layer to form a lining. Use plastic sheeting on top.

Coir/coconut fiber Usually shaped into a thick circular mat with slits cut into the rim

Above: Recycled felt or wool liners are not the most attractive you can buy, but they retain moisture well and are relatively inexpensive. Use them when you are sure the liner will not be visible once the basket is completed!

Above: *Conifer clippings are an attractive, natural alternative to the many manufactured linings. Use plastic sheeting on top to retain water.*

for easy fitting. It is a renewable resource and looks fairly natural even though it's brown in color. Loose coconut fibre, sometimes dyed green, can be used in the same way as moss.

Felt/recycled wool A cheap lining material with a soft, woolly texture that absorbs moisture.

Sponge Liners are often recycled from chips of plastic foam. They absorb moisture, helping to keep the compost damp, but are not very attractive.

Plastic sheeting Cheap and versatile. Line wire baskets with black or green refuse sack plastic or thicker plastic compost sacks. Slit holes in the sides to allow for planting. It is surprisingly unobtrusive.

COMPOSTS
Soil-less composts These can be made from peat, recycled materials, or coir, and are

much lighter than soil-based composts which are not normally used for baskets.

Peat A multi-purpose peat-based compost is fine for baskets but there will only be sufficient fertilizer for six to eight weeks,

Below: *Black plastic is probably the cheapest and most versatile of all liners for baskets.*

necessitating feeding. These composts may dry out and be difficult to re-wet. Special hanging basket composts contain slow-release fertilizer granules and a chemical designed to keep the growing medium moist.

Coir A natural by-product from the coconut industry. The compost made from it has low moisture-retention properties and fertilizers may leach out of the compost with frequent watering. Use a special coir fertilizer.

Recycled compost Less readily available and can be variable in quality, but it is a "green" material and worth experimenting with.

Above: *Mix slow-release fertilizer into compost to avoid having to feed later on.*

PREPARING YOUR BASKET

Once you have selected your liner and growing medium, it is time to begin preparing
your basket. As with so many things, in this discipline preparation is all. A well-planned
and correctly formulated basket can give you months of trouble-free pleasure,
but cut corners at this stage and you might come to regret it.

*10 Point Plan for Planting a Traditional
Basket*

1. Bring all your "ingredients" together,
   ready prepared, along with your utensils
   —pre-soaked plants, moist compost
   (perhaps with some slow-release
   fertilizer mixed in), basket, and liner.

2. Chains get in the way of working, so if
   they will come off (try pliers), it will
   make things easier for you.

3. Conventional hanging baskets will roll
   around unless you steady them in a large
   plant pot. Wall baskets also need support
   to keep them upright while working.

4. If you are using a traditional wire basket
   and moss, fill the base of the basket
   with well-soaked moss. Place on top a
   plastic pot saucer to act as a reservoir.
   Alternatively, use a piece of black plastic
   about the size of a dinner plate. Add
   another ring of moss to build up the sides,
   then fill this base with planting medium.

5. Use small rooted cuttings or "plugs" with
   a root mass small enough to fit through
   the wire mesh. Either wrap fragile stems
   in a tube of newspaper and feed the

*Left: Whichever lining you opt
to use, offer it up to the basket
and carefully trim it to fit with
scissors, allowing for the liner to
slip down a little once the
growing medium and plants
have been added.*

*Left: Tuck the prepared lining
snugly into position all around
your basket and, if necessary,
add a second water-retaining
liner over the top of the first.*

plant through from the inside or simply force the rootball through from the outside. Make sure the plant is well inside the basket then pack the neck of the plant round with moss. Continue round in this way and then cover the ring of rootballs with more compost. Gradually build up the sides, alternating the position of the plants so that the area is evenly covered.

6. When using a plastic sheet liner, hold the edge in place with clothes pins and begin to fill the basket up with layers of compost and plants, cutting a small slit for each plant. Push the rootball through using a pencil or dibber.

7. If you plant trailers in the top of the basket, around the rim, there is no need to cover the sides completely. Tilt the plant so that the stems are already hanging over the edge, but make sure the top of the rootball is covered with compost. Put the central specimen plant in next and fill the space in between with smaller bushy plants.

8. Fit a watering funnel made from the inverted top half of a transparent plastic soda or water bottle. Place the funnel as close to the center as possible and bury the base with compost.

9. If you do not want to use liquid feed throughout the growing season, and have not already mixed in powdered or granular slow-release fertilizer, push in fertilizer sticks or tabs according to manufacturer's instructions.

10. Water thoroughly using a fine rose attachment on your watering can.

Aim to ensure that your liner is evenly distributed across and around the basket, so that soil and moisture will be retained well throughout the basket.

Once you are satisfied that your liner fits well, is evenly distributed, and will securely hold your materials, add the growing medium and begin planting up. Follow the instructions opposite for the general principles of planting up hanging baskets.

19

CHOOSING YOUR PLANTS

It is plants that make hanging baskets striking. No matter how stylish the basket
you select or the materials you line it with, it is what you choose to plant
in it that will govern whether or not your basket is a success.

BUYING AT THE GARDEN CENTER

Bedding and patio plants This is the category in which most summer basket plants can be found. In recent years there's been a huge increase in the range of material available. Some of the new arrivals represent a significant improvement while others are more like novelty items—fun to experiment with, but don't risk basing your whole display on them!

Early start Half-hardy annuals and tender perennials in the form of seedlings, plugs, or young plants are available from late winter to midspring. But you will need a warm, light spot to grow them on until they are ready to move outdoors, and that could mean up to four months, depending on time of purchase. If you have the facilities, this is the cheapest way to plant a basket, short of raising your own from seeds and cuttings. Prick out seedlings and pot on plantlets as soon as you get them home. Alternatively, plant up your basket straightaway (plugs make planting up the sides of wire baskets very simple), and grow on in a heated greenhouse or conservatory.

Instant baskets From midspring to mid-summer, bedding, and patio plants are available in a very wide range of sizes, from small plants in modular trays to individually potted plants including larger specimens. You will have more choice at the start of the season and plants also tend to be in better condition when they first arrive. Varieties sold as single color strains are useful for co-ordinating arrangements and F1 hybrids, although more expensive, tend to ensure greater consistency and performance over F2

Above: Verbena *"Raspberry Crush"* is a reliable and attractive all-purpose plant for hanging baskets and wall containers.

Left: Fuchsias are classic bedding plants that can be bought widely and inexpensively as rooted cuttings in spring.

Above: Coleus *has vivid foliage but needs some shelter to perform well.*

or nutrient deficiency. Spots and yellow streaking on foliage indicate disease or viral infection.

• Avoid plants that have been cut back or have had old flowers trimmed off—they have probably been hanging around for some time.

• Avoid seedlings and plants that are pale and drawn. They will have been weakened through growing in poor light levels.

• Do not buy plants that are displayed in exposed conditions outdoors during cold periods in spring. They may look fine, but could later show signs of chilling injury.

• Avoid plants with wilted shoots and dry soil. Erratic watering may have damaged their root systems.

• Avoid pot-bound plants where a mass of roots fills the pot and protrudes through the

and open-pollinated kinds. Starter kits that include a range of basket plants in a single pack are useful if you are just starting out or if you only want a small quantity. If you have nowhere to keep plants or newly planted baskets under cover while there is still a risk of frost, then it's best to plant later using more mature material for an instant display.

BUYING TIPS

• Choose good, bushy plants, well-clothed in leaves that have not yet started to flower, or with plenty of flower buds and just one or two open blooms.

• Unless they are variegated, plants should be a healthy green with no yellowing. Red, brown, or purple tinting may indicate chilling

Above: *When you select your plants, always think carefully about the end results. You should aim for a well-balanced, appealing spread of colors and form.*

21

drainage holes. Equally, be suspicious of compost with very few roots visible—it could be a sign of vine weevil or some other root problem, such as overwatering.

• Check plants thoroughly for signs of pests and diseases before purchase. The white discarded skins of aphids are easier to spot than the living insects. Under glass, whitefly could also have taken hold—you will notice these as tiny, white, triangular insects that fly up when foliage is disturbed. Fuchsias are a favorite. Do not buy from places infested with whitefly, as the pest is very difficult to eradicate, even with chemical sprays.

• If you are unsure, ask the staff when it will be safe to move the plants outdoors permanently in your area. Also note that in fall and winter, plants such as primroses are sometimes displayed outdoors but may only be suitable for very sheltered positions and for indoor use.

Alternatives to bedding You can include all kinds of plants in baskets and wall planters —there really is no need to stick to bedding or patio plants. And from midsummer onward you will almost certainly need to look in other sections of your garden center or nursery to find a big enough range of fresh

Above: Gazania *"Daybreak"*—a low growing tender perennial, grown as an annual, works well in hanging baskets and pots in full sun.

Below: The leaves of this lamium would brighten a shady spot.

plant material to fill a basket. Later in the year you will need to look even farther afield.

Herbs Many ornamental varieties are now available, and types with colored or variegated foliage combine beautifully with flowering bedding. Try the variegated and colored leaf sages, thymes, and mints, as well as golden marjoram and purple-leaf basil. For fall and winter baskets, small pots of rosemary, and silver-leaved herbs like lavender, cotton lavender (*Santolina*), and curry plant are useful.

Herbaceous perennials Compact-growing perennials with handsome foliage such as purple-leaved heucheras and golden creeping Jenny (*Lysimachia nummularia* "Aurea") make good mixers with flowering

bedding. You can also try plants producing a profusion of blooms such as the carpeting campanulas and some of the hardy geraniums. These can be planted out in the garden at the end of the season.

Alpines Several strong-growing alpines and rock-garden plants are suitable for baskets. One of the best is *Rhodanthemum hosmariense*, with silver, feathery foliage, and large, white, daisy blooms produced over a very long period. Sedums and thymes have good drought resistance, and along with ajugas are useful for covering the sides of baskets.

Evergreen shrubs These are particularly useful for winter baskets and can often be purchased as young plants in fall

Above: Santolina chamaecyparissus *(cotton lavender) has a dense, rounded habit and striking foliage ideal for hanging baskets. and wall containers.*

Above: Rhodanthemum hosmariense *produces cheerful daisy blooms over a long period and has interesting foliage.*

23

specifically for this purpose. Variegated *Euonymus fortunei* cultivars give a bright splash of color, as do certain berrying shrubs such as *Gaultheria mucronata* and skimmias. Mix them with evergreen herbs, alpines, and ivies for creative displays.

Houseplants During summer, all kinds of foliage houseplants can be mixed into hanging baskets, including trailing tradescantias,

Ivies of all varieties are useful as trailers and for mixing in with plants for creative displays.

asparagus ferns, coleus (*Solenostemon*) and spider plants (*Chlorophytum*). Fall and winter baskets can also be supplemented, provided plants have been hardened off properly. Try winter cherry (*Solanum*), mini chrysanthemums and mini cyclamen.

Buying mail order There are several advantages to buying seedlings, rooted cuttings, plugs and young plants by post. You need to get your orders in early, but it allows you to:

• Try out new varieties before they are available in garden centers.

• Make an early start if young plants and seedlings are not available locally.

• Save money by using rooted cuttings as opposed to larger pot-grown plants.

• Cut out the problem of plants that are very difficult to germinate, such as begonia and impatiens, which are available as seedlings or plugs.

The main disadvantage is that plants can suffer with delays or damage in transit. You must also be prepared to deal with plants immediately they arrive.

***Right:** This superb hanging basket features fuchsias as its centerpiece, mixed with ivy, striking silver foliage, and a variety of bedding plants. It has been strategically hung to decorate the bare wall of a shed.*

***Below:** Impatiens "Super Elfin" has beautiful flowers but is difficult to germinate.*

COLOR GUIDE (1)

The next few pages are designed to give you ideas of how best to combine colors in your hanging baskets. Firstly, how to mix blues and purples in the most successful combinations.

Impatiens *(busy Lizzie)* "Mosaic Lilac" offers subtle purple-pink tones that blend well with stronger hues.

STYLING YOUR BASKET

You can create all kinds of different effects by combining certain shades or by restricting your choice of flower and foliage to a single colorway. If you are not sure which plants work well together, keeping color schemes simple is a recipe for success. The end result can be dramatic, elegant, or contemporary depending on what shades you decide to use in your basket arrangements.

RICH AND VIBRANT

Certain deep, velvety purples and the vivid purple-reds such as cerise and magenta combine perfectly with purple-blues. These shades can be found in many summer flowers including…

Fuchsias
Geraniums
Heliotrope "Marine"
Impatiens (busy Lizzie)
Petunias
Verbenas

…and in winter, blooms of pansies and violas, as well as those of primrose and polyanthus, especially the jewel-like Wanda hybrids. Put a real zing in the display by adding a hint of lemon yellow, or orange.

BLUES AND PURPLES

There are many shades of lilac- and lavender-blue or purple-flowered bedding and patio plants. But there are few true blues such as gentian or sky blue, apart from felicias, violas, and pansies. Blues and purples complement yellows and lime greens and help to cool down hot colors.

Ageratum *"Blue Danube"* has rich blue tones and soft texture that complement larger blooms well.

PASTEL PURPLES AND BLUES

Ageratum
Brachyscome multifida "Blue Mist"
Campanula isophylla "Stella"
Convolvulus sabatius
Fuchsias, e.g., "La Campanella"
Impatiens "Blue Pearl"
Laurentia "Blue Stars"
Lobelia erinus (trailing e.g. "Lilac Cascade," and bush forms)
Nemesia caerulea "Elliot's Variety" and "Joan Wilder"
Petunias
Scaevola aemula "Blue Wonder"
Sutera cordata "Lilac Pearls"
Verbenas
Violas

Left: Verbena *"Sissinghurst"* has vivid pink blooms that combine perfectly with deep purples and pastel blues.

Left: Viola × wittrockiana *"Impressions Blue Shades"* produces blooms in cool water colors and is perfect for shade.

Above: Lobelia *"Cascade"* is a superb plant for hanging baskets, with a dramatic, tumbling habit, and varied tones of purple, blue, and white.

DEEP BLUES AND PURPLES

Ageratums
Fuchsias
Heliotrope "Marine"
Impatiens (busy Lizzie)
Lobelia erinus (trailing, and bush forms)
Petunias (especially the trailing Surfinia group)
Verbenas, e.g., "Homestead Purple" and "Tapien Violet"
Violas

HOT SPOTS

Finally, metallic bronze-purples create the illusion of heat, and look wonderful against a red-brick wall. Try them in terracotta-colored baskets and wall containers for a Mediterranean look. Good plants include: Basil "Purple Ruffles" and *Heuchera* "Palace Purple."

Above: Brachyscome *"Blue Mist"* forms mossy hummocks covered in soft blue daisies.

27

COLOR GUIDE (2)

Pastel schemes have always been popular for baskets and containers with so many soft pinks and lilac-blues to choose from, and in recent years plant breeders have tended toward more subtle and romantic colorings.

PRETTY PASTELS

You will find many pastel mixtures among plants like pansies, impatiens, and lobelia and bedding with beautifully shaded and edged petals.

Arrangements can be rather insipid unless lots of lush greenery, some white flowers, and a few stronger colors are peppered in. Try deep purples, crimson, and cerise pinks for contrast. One alternative is to mix pinks with soft apricot and peach, using silver and white or lime green as a neutral background. Another is to combine pale yellow, cream and silver with touches of lilac and lavender.

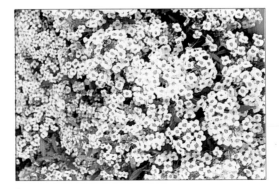

Lobularia *"Snow Crystals" (white alyssum) makes a delicate froth of white that works well filling in a pastel display in a hanging basket.*

PALE PINKS

Begonia sempervirens
Begonia (tuberous-rooted)
Brachyscome "Pink Mist"
Diascia
Fuchsia
Geranium
Impatien
Petunia
Verbena

SILVERS, GRAYS AND WHITES

Argyranthemum	*Petunia*
Begonia (tuberous-rooted)	*Plecostachys serpyllifolia*
Fuchsia	*Rhodanthemum hosmariense*
Geranium	*Santolina chamaecyparissus*
Helichrysum petiolare	(cotton lavender)
Impatien	*Senecio cineraria* "Silver
Lobularia "Snow Crystals"	Dust" and "Cirrus"
Osteospermum	*Sutera cordata* "Snowflake"
Pansies/violas	*Verbena*

AIR OF ELEGANCE

White and silver baskets have an air of distinction and are easy to put together successfully. They work particularly well with white-painted woodwork and metalwork and hung from buildings with classical proportions where they can be used to create a rhythm across the façade. To enhance the display still further, add just a touch of pink, or salmon and lime green. For a shady spot, to add a note of purity, try white flowers with green and white variegated foliage and apricot-pink highlights.

Above: *The delicate apricot-pink of this* Begonia × tuberhybrida *contrasts well with other pastels and stronger colors. Large-flowered doubles also provide strong upright form for hanging baskets and wall containers.*

Above: Diascia *"Ruby Fields" produces tubular, salmon-pink flowers throughout summer and has a slightly trailing habit.*

Above: Argyranthemum frutescens *(marguerite) has bright white, yellow, or pink daisy-like flowers that thrust upward toward the sun.*

Left: Cineraria *"Silver Dust" has lacy silver foliage that adds elegance to baskets of pale pastel flowers.*

29

COLOR GUIDE (3)

Yellows and creams add sunshine and combine effectively with many other colors. Don't forget variegated foliage and feel free to experiment with more daring, contemporary schemes.

COOL AND REFRESHING

Citrus shades of lemon yellow, clear orange, and lime green make a mouth-watering display. Avoid silver foliage and instead use plenty of greenery and yellow- or white-variegated foliage and orange-leaved coleus (*Solenostemon*). Blue stains and paints for woodwork and walls are very popular, and this refreshing color scheme looks stunning against such a backdrop.

Asteriscus maritimus *has circular blooms that are perfectly complemented by the foliage.*

YELLOWS AND CREAMS

Asteriscus maritimus
Begonia (tuberous)
Bidens ferulifolia
Brachycome "Lemon Mist"
Calceolaria "Sunshine"
Osteospermum, e.g., "Buttermilk"
Lysimachia congestiflora
Lysimachia nummularia
Marigold
Mimulus
Nasturtium
Pansy/Viola
Petunia, e.g. "Prism Sunshine" F1
Tagetes "Lemon Gem"

YELLOW- AND WHITE-VARIEGATED FOLIAGE

Chlorophytum comosum (spider plant)
Euonymus fortunei cultivars
Felicia amelloides "Variegata"
Glechoma hederacea "Variegata"
Hedera helix (variegated English ivy)
Helichrysum petiolare "Variegata"
Lamium maculatum, e.g. "White Nancy'
Nasturtium "Alaska"
Plectranthus forsteri "Marginatus"
Salvia officinalis "Icterina"
Sedum lineare "Variegatum"

Begonias come in a variety of shades and often have attractive tinting and shading.

Bidens ferulifolia *"Golden Eye" has starry blooms and attractive, feathery foliage.*

CONTEMPORARY

Bright, but simple, combinations tend to have a modern look. Try lime green with a fizzy, day-glow pink or a combination of white flowers and white or yellow variegated foliage shot through with cerise or magenta. Pair up true-blues with lemon yellows and lime foliage and combine deep velvet purples with scarlet, and splashes of silver. An alternative approach is to go for a more subtle, minimalist feel. Try gray, metallic containers with lavender, cream, and silver planting or silvers, grays, and palest purples with a contrast of purple-blacks, and deep, blood red.

LIME GREEN FOLIAGE
Solenostemon (Coleus)
Fuchsia, e.g., "Golden Marinka"
Geranium
Hedera helix (English ivy)
Helichrysum petiolare "Limelight"
Lamium maculatum "Aureum"
Lysimachia nummularia "Aurea"
Tanacetum parthenium "Aureum"
(golden feverfew)
Thymes

VIVID PURPLE-PINKS
Fuchsias
Geraniums
Impatiens
Lobelia, e.g., "Rosamund"
Petunias
Primroses (hybrid)
Portulacas
Verbenas

Above: *Every now and again it is a good idea to break up your combinations of creams, yellows, and greens with plants that feature natural dark highlights, such as Tagetes "Naughty Marietta."*

Below: *Alternatively, you can reverse your main and highlighted colors, as in this dark viola, with its brilliant yellow center.*

Above: Tagetes *"Yellow Jacket"* could offer an interesting variation of form in an all-yellow basket with its large rounded flower heads.

31

ESTABLISHING YOUR BASKET

Once you have selected your baskets, chosen your plants, and thought about everything from liners and composts to color combinations, it is time to begin getting your plantings properly established.

Many of us like to plant our baskets up early, using young plants and rooted cuttings, but outdoors in late spring, conditions are far too cold to hang them straight out. You'll need somewhere reasonably warm, light, and sheltered to grow them on for several weeks until night time temperatures rise and summer begins in earnest. You can then begin the gradual process of hardening off.

Above: *Preparing and rejuvenating baskets in a greenhouse. Keep plants undercover until you are absolutely sure it is safe to put them outdoors.*

Even if the plants you have used are reasonably mature and fully hardened off—that is, acclimatized to outdoor conditions, there are still things you can do to encourage rapid establishment.

PREPARING FOR DIFFICULT CONDITIONS

The walls of a house actually present quite a hostile environment for plants. Buildings tend to generate wind turbulence which can snap off brittle shoots. Windy conditions can cause soft shoot tips to wither through rapid dehydration and new plants without a well-established root system will struggle to grow as they may be unable to take up sufficient water. Bright sunlight may scorch young shoots and the heat radiated back onto the basket from a sun-baked wall adds to the problem of water loss and low humidity.

FASTER GROWTH UNDER GLASS

Rather than hang the basket straight away in its permanent position, consider growing the arrangement on in a greenhouse, cold frame

Above: *When you are getting your baskets established, avoid exposed walls where bright sunlight and wind can cause extensive damage.*

Above: Most baskets will fit easily into the top of a standard bucket for soaking.

or well-ventilated glass porch. A couple of weeks under cover, especially at the start of the summer season when the nights may still be quite cold, will help the basket fill out more quickly. The warm, humid conditions will also promote root growth, helping the plants to survive the rigors of outdoor life more easily.

SHELTERED SPOT OUTDOORS

Alternatively, stand baskets in the tops of buckets or large flowerpots and keep in a sheltered spot out of midday sun during the day. Bring the baskets under cover at night, especially if there is the slightest chance of frost. A shed or garage will be fine. This is also the best way to gradually acclimatize baskets made up from plants that have previously only been grown indoors or under glass. Start with just two or three hours and build up slowly.

FEEDING

Spray foliage with a balanced foliar feed containing trace elements while the baskets are being grown on under glass or being hardened off ready for hanging. This helps to build up their strength and encourage bushy, healthy growth.

Above: A well-established wall manger. If you are not sure how well established your basket is, or are unable to keep plants under glass, hang it in a sheltered corner.

Above: Regular feeding of plant foliage with a balanced foliar spray-feed will encourage vigorous growth, reduce the risk of pests and diseases, and later help the plant protect itself from the vagaries of the weather.

WHERE AND HOW
TO HANG YOUR BASKET

After all the work involved in preparing your basket, you need to give careful consideration as to where to hang it in order for it to have the maximum effect. There are a number of points to bear in mind.

When hanging a basket you need to consider practicality and safety, aesthetics, and the needs of your plants. Do not hang baskets where people will knock their heads as they walk past, or so close to the doorway that you have to fight your way through trailing foliage to get in and out—remember, baskets can grow considerably bigger than when first planted! If there is not much room to maneuver, consider wall pots and baskets as a space-saving alternative.

You do not have to hang baskets from traditional brackets: this can really restrict where you put them. To hang from a pergola or porch, all you need to do is to screw sturdy hooks into the woodwork. Custom-built wall baskets usually come with screw holes, but you can also fix ordinary round plant pots to the wall or drainpipes, using specially designed clips which are readily available.

Where you position baskets can make all the difference to how easy they are to maintain and how well the plants perform. Baskets will certainly need almost

Left: Allow plenty of room to accommodate trailing plants. Single-subject baskets like this superb cascading petunia can be very effective, but must be grown to perfection as there are no other plants to distract the eye.

Above: These cleverly designed coach lamps have hooks which allow hanging baskets to be suspended underneath. At night, the flowers will be illuminated, making a real welcome for visitors.

daily attention—feeding, watering, dead-heading—so hang them for easy access or fit pulleys for raising and lowering. Keep plants with similar requirements for light and moisture together so that you can hang them where they will have the optimum conditions for growth.

Above: *This symmetrically planted wall basket, hung on a central pillar between two doorways, emphasizes the architectural detail perfectly. Select plants with the site of the basket in mind.*

Below: *The traditional way to hang baskets is from a bracket fixed to a wall or fence. Brackets come in many different designs and can be simple or highly ornamented.*

FIXING A BRACKET TO A WALL

As a matter of safety, it is important that you fix hanging basket brackets properly. When attaching a bracket, you need to plug the hole to prevent the screw from working its way out (see below). Always use the correct size bracket for the basket. These are usually sold for a particular basket diameter, say 12 or 14 inches.

1 *Put the bracket against the wall and mark the position of the screw holes using a felt tipped pen. Using a hammer-action drill and the correct sized bit, drill the top hole.*

2 *Push the wall plug into the hole, then put the bracket back in place and loosely fix the screw in to check the position of the second hole.*

3 *Drill and plug the second hole and screw the bracket firmly in place. For wall pots and baskets, follow the same steps for drilling and plugging.*

FEEDING AND WATERING

Watering should be a daily or, better still, twice daily routine, especially for baskets
hung in full sun or a windy spot. Never rely on rainfall to do the job for you,
and don't wait for plants to wilt before attending to them.

Some basket plants never fully recover and soil-less compost is notoriously difficult to re-wet once it has dried beyond a certain point. Fortunately, there are several ways to make the job easier. You can buy easy-reach attachments for hose pipes or devices which allow you to raise or lower a basket for maintenance.

The trick is to apply a slow and steady stream of water so that it has a chance to really soak in. Don't assume that just because water starts running out that the basket has reached capacity. It is more effective if you use a small watering can to apply several doses through the day, than giving baskets a quick deluge, which inevitably results in the water pouring

Left: Water can be made to seep slowly into the basket via a mini reservoir sunk into the compost. Cut a plastic soda bottle in half and bury the pointed end in the compost at planting time. It will soon be camouflaged as the plants grow.

straight out. Use 14- or 16-inch diameter baskets in preference to 12-inch ones, unless you can guarantee adequate watering, and choose self-watering baskets if you are unable to water daily in summer.

Once the feed in the potting mix has been used up (see back of bag for timings), begin to apply liquid feeds usually once a week at full strength or every time you water using roughly half the recommended dose. Too much leafy growth at the expense of flowers usually means that you are using a product with too high a proportion of Nitrogen. Choose a fertilizer recommended for bedding and other flowering plants.

Bottom left: Regular liquid feeding gives the best results, but if you don't have the time, or are apt to forget, then use slow-release feeding pellets or tablets such as the Osmocote pellets shown here. These are inserted into the compost at planting time and last the whole season. Feed is released when plants are watered, the amount varying according to temperature.

Easy-to-operate pulley systems which clip onto the hanging hook or bracket allow for easy access to baskets for feeding, watering, and maintenance.

SOAKING A DRIED-OUT HANGING BASKET

1 Water just runs straight through a dried-out basket. Add detergent to help the water "stick" to the soil.

2 Plunge the basket in the water and leave until the mix is saturated. Drain, and then let the plants recover.

Reach up to the base of the basket and pull it down when you want to attend to the plants. Afterward, nudge the basket up to release the lock, and push it back into position.

An empty plastic bottle is also a useful aid to watering, especially if you just have one or two baskets. It is much lighter than a full watering can and is therefore ideal for overhead watering.

VACATION CARE FOR HANGING BASKETS

Hanging baskets are generally sensitive things that require plenty of
loving care and attention in order to thrive. However, hardly anybody
has unlimited time to devote to plant care, and what do you do
if you are going away for the weekend or on vacation?

The best solution to the problem of how to look after hanging baskets is a willing neighbor! If you can't arrange for someone to stand in for you until your return, then you'll need to make other provisions. One of the first steps is to soak baskets so that the soil is saturated with water, then put them down in a shady spot at floor level. Up on the wall they are much more exposed to drying elements—wind, sun and heat radiated back onto the basket from the wall. This procedure should keep baskets in reasonable condition for three or four days unless the weather is exceptionally hot. Even if someone is coming in to water, it is a good idea to do this, clustering the baskets together in one place to allow easy access.

For longer periods, a little more preparation is required. "Planting" baskets in a shady border is a good solution for maintaining traditional baskets lined with moss or another porous material (see below). Moisture-loss is dramatically

USING A CAPILLARY WICK

Cut a piece of capillary matting into a long strip. Soak it in water, then push one end well into the soil of the basket and leave the other end in a container of water. Set the apparatus up a couple of days before you leave to check that water is being taken up by the plants.

reduced when the sides of the basket are surrounded by damp soil. Another technique is to set up some kind of automatic watering system connected to an outside tap fitted with a timer. You can also use the capillary wick method illustrated. This is ideal for wall pots and baskets with solid sides. Whatever method you choose, remove flowers which will be over by your return, and deal with any pest problems before you leave.

3 *Sprinkle a few slug pellets into and around the hole and in the top of the basket to help protect against attack. Check carefully for slugs.*

Baskets sunk into damp soil and surrounded by plants in a shady border will lose water much less rapidly than if left on a wall

5 *It may seem like a rather drastic measure, but it is essential that all flowers are removed. Bunch together stems of small-flowered plants and cut back near the base.*

1 *Find a spot in a sheltered shady part of the garden and dig a hole large enough to accommodate the base of the basket up to the level of planting.*

4 *Lifting trailers clear of the base, lower the basket into the prepared hole. Arrange the hanging chain to rest on the surface, then backfill with soil.*

2 *Water the hole thoroughly and at the same time soak the basket in readiness for planting. You need to ensure maximum saturation before you go away.*

6 *Take off any flowers which will be over by the time you return—usually any bloom which has started to open.*

A BACKDROP FOR A BASKET

Hanging baskets are often used to disguise bare walls or eyesores, and certainly they can serve a useful role in this respect. However, whenever possible it is good to think of your basket as a *complement* to its backdrop, and plan it accordingly.

The success of any hanging basket display is closely tied in with the backdrop you select. Backgrounds can be neutral-colored, complementary, or contrasting. You can hang most baskets against white-washed or light pastel-colored rendering and woodwork, gray stone, or weathered fencing. Brickwork is more tricky—it comes in all shades, and the orange-red end of the spectrum makes a particularly difficult backdrop, especially for certain pink flower shades. In this case it is best to stick to other "hot" colors—flame reds, oranges, and golden yellows—or contrasting "cool" silver-grays, blues, purples, and white. These hot and cool colors also work well when mixed together. Another alternative for difficult or unattractive backdrops is to create your own. Fix trellis panels to the wall and paint or stain an appropriate color, then fix brackets above or through the panels so that the flowers and foliage hang down over the new backdrop.

Some of the strongest visual effects come from linking the color of basket plants to a color used in the background. This includes minor detailing, such as an attractively colored front door or window shutters. Try

Left: This mix of salmon-pink geraniums, busy Lizzy, and blue lobelia is perfectly complemented by the pale brick backdrop. The same scheme would not have worked so well against a red brick wall.

Left: Baskets can look beautiful hung on a climber-clad wall, all the more so when the flowers and foliage of the backdrop match the basket color scheme. Here lilac pink impatiens team up with purple clematis.

complementing white-washed walls and woodwork with mixed baskets of silver, blue, lilac, and white or contrast blue paintwork with yellow, orange, cerise pink, or red schemes.

Plain greenery makes an ideal foil for colorful mixed baskets and it is well worth fixing hanging brackets on climber-clad walls and fences. If the foliage backdrop is variegated, pick strong colors and bold foliage so that the basket really stands out. For a more subtle effect, try matching or toning basket plants with the flowers of a climber or wall shrub.

Below: A small basket adds a splash of vibrant color to a shady wall. Without flowers, this white-washed wall could have looked rather dull until the pyracantha berries developed their color in early fall.

Left: Here, matching arrangements of cherry-red trailing begonias, blue lobelia, and sharp lime green lysimachia make a strong contrast to a starkly painted black-and-white entrance.

Tuberous begonias and trailing lobelia are happy in a shady, sheltered spot

MAKING AN IMPACT WITH BASKETS

Hanging baskets and wall containers are designed primarily to be decorative objects. There is little point in creating a stark or minimalist basket, as it simply will not attract much attention. Nine times out of ten, the whole objective of designing and creating hanging containers should be to make as big a visual impact as possible.

No matter how tiny a backyard you have, there will always be space for hanging baskets. Even if the ground is paved, bare walls and fences can be instantly transformed into a hanging garden. In a new plot where

Above: *Hanging baskets provide extra growing space for flowers in this small patio garden. The baskets are an integral part of the scheme and, along with other climbers and wall plants, succeed in creating a colorful facade for the surrounding fencing.*

climbers and wall shrubs are still very small, trailing foliage from hanging baskets can cover the gaps easily and basket blooms provide a continuation of color from the border up. Baskets and wall pots can also be used to draw the eye toward an attractive feature, such as a house name plate, or a decorative window.

There are a number of ways to make such vertical displays even more eye-catching.

Above: *Ivy-leaved geraniums (pelargoniums), verbena, and diascia in rich pinks and reds are contrasted with deep blue lobelia in these matching baskets. Hung side by side, the plants grow and merge together, forming what looks at first sight to be a single large basket, perfectly in scale with the surrounding architecture.*

Above: There is no law which dictates that hanging baskets have to be suspended at head height. Here color is brought right up to the front door by filling the gaps at the end of the window troughs with hanging baskets hung at the same level.

Hang an identical basket on either side of a doorway, and straightaway you have doubled the dramatic effect. If two or three baskets are grouped very close to one another, you can persuade people into thinking that it is just one enormous arrangement. And, with several baskets hanging in a line, it is possible to create a continuous ribbon of color. This technique is all the more effective if the basket plants are chosen to fit into a particular color scheme or if an identical variety is used throughout. (Pick a reliable variety such as Swiss balcony geraniums). You can strengthen the design further by mirroring the planting in windowboxes, pots, and planters in the rest of the garden. A variation on the theme is to hang baskets between windowboxes, forming an unbroken line of flowers.

Above: Simple color schemes often create the strongest impact. Here, vibrant red contrasts with the pale stone and Mediterranean-blue paintwork. The trailing geraniums in hanging baskets form a band of flowers across the front of the house and the effect is strengthened by using the same color for the troughs and planters below.

Below: The eye is immediately drawn to these cottage-style windows divided by the abundant flowers of this collection of large and small hanging baskets. The planting is so dense that the plain red brickwork between the white-framed windows is almost completely obscured. Baskets positioned in such a way provide a visual treat both for visitors approaching the house and for those looking out of the windows from the inside. An additional bonus might be flower fragrance from the baskets wafting through the open windows.

THE PROJECTS

Spring Projects 46

Summer Projects 64

Fall Projects 94

Winter Projects 102

45

A SELF-WATERING SPRING BASKET

For people who are out of the house all day or who are a little forgetful when it comes to watering, a self-watering hanging basket is the perfect solution. It reduces the risk of plants drying out or dying due to unintentional neglect, and keeps your hanging basket looking its best at all times of day.

Immediately after planting, water the basket in the normal way to ensure that the compost is thoroughly wetted. Thereafter, water will be drawn up from the reservoir at the bottom of the basket, as and when the plants require it. If you use the tube to fill the reservoir, there is no danger of overwatering, as seep holes in the sides allow the excess to drain out.

As a contrast to the dark green basket, for this project a fresh scheme of yellow and white spring flowers and foliage was chosen. As it has solid sides, all of the planting has to go in the top of the basket, so pick at least one plant with long trails to soften the edge. This green and white variegated ivy with its finely pointed leaves stands out beautifully.

White drumstick primulas pick up on the white-edged ivy and make a striking and unusual centerpiece. Their display is relatively long-lived, the spherical heads

1 *A wick draws water up from the reservoir at the base of the basket, keeping the sheet of capillary matting inside it constantly damp, and hence the soil which is in contact with it. Feed the wick through the plastic base plate. Push the watering tube through the hole in the base plate, before you begin adding potting mix and plants. You should be able to camouflage it easily.*

Use a peat-based hanging basket compost

2 *Add a layer of moist potting mixture, covering the capillary matting completely.*

3 *If the rootball of your plant is too big to fit the basket, knock off any loose soil and tease the roots of the plant apart at the base so that they spread out flat.*

opening and developing over a number of weeks. When flowering has finished, transfer the plants to the garden.

The strongly shaped and glossy-leafed *Euonymus japonicus* "Aureus" was bought from a garden center as little pots of rooted cuttings. When this basket is dismantled, it should be possible to separate these out and pot them up individually.

6 *Split a couple of pots of rooted ivy cuttings, and fit around the top edge of the basket. Fill any gaps with soil and water the potting mix.*

4 *Add another drumstick primula and then fill in the gaps left on one side with the variegated euonymus. Put in more potting mix.*

5 *Plant two hardy primroses, one on either side of the watering tube, leaving sufficient room around the rim for some trailing plants.*

Primula denticulata "Alba" *(white-flowered drumstick primula)*

Euonymus japonicus "Aureus"

Primula *(hardy hybrid primrose)*

Hedera helix *cultivar (variegated ivy)*

7 *Hang the basket in a lightly shaded, sheltered spot. Remove individual blooms as they fade and cut off drumsticks when the whole head has finished flowering.*

HYACINTHS AND PRIMULAS

This scheme is a rich blend of jewel-colored primulas, red hyacinths, and warm terracotta, shades more often associated with late summer. It will bring welcome color and style to any wall in spring, and can be easily adapted using the many different colors in which hyacinths and primulas now come.

The new *Primula* "Wanda" hybrids have introduced a whole set of colors for the spring garden—glowing purples, reds, and blues, which are often farther enhanced by dark foliage. Mixed trays of plants may contain white-, yellow-, and pink-flowered forms, so if you want to copy this scheme, wait until one or two buds have opened to check the color or buy plants separately in flower.

Headily scented hyacinths can often be bought in bud as single bulbs and add a luxurious touch to plantings of this kind. Like the hybrid primroses, hyacinths now come in many different colors, including orange, and creamy yellow, though as potted bulbs, pinks, blues, and white still predominate. The advantage of buying plants in single colors is of course that color scheming in mixed arrangements is so much easier.

3 *Place the hyacinths against the back wall of the basket, leaving space for the primulas in the foreground. You may need to shake off some of the potting mix from around the roots to create more room.*

1 *Line the wall basket with black plastic. Cut a hole in the base by the drainage hole. Put a flat stone over the hole to prevent soil loss. Add a layer of gravel to provide good drainage.*

Make sure that the potting mix is moistened before use

2 *Cover the gravel with some potting mixture. Always use fresh potting mix and never garden compost or soil straight from your backyard, as it contains too many pests and diseases.*

4 *Don't worry if the hyacinths look a little awkward at first; the primroses will soon cover up the base of the bulbs. Lay the plants out first, so that you can work out which are the best color combinations.*

5 *Squeeze the rootballs into an oval shape so that you can fit in as many plants as possible. Winter and spring baskets tend not to grow like summer ones, so they need to be crammed full for maximum impact.*

MORE SPRING SCHEMES

- Silver cineraria, pale blue pansies, white polyanthus
- Velvet-red pansies, *Heuchera* "Palace Purple" centerpiece, dark green ivy trails
- White heather, *Lamium* "White Nancy"
- Red bellis (double daisies), *Festuca glauca* centerpiece
- Slate-blue polyanthus, cream violas, *Euonymus japonicus* "Aureus"

There are several ways to approach color scheming, all of which can produce very effective results. One is to stick to just one color of flower, but to vary the form and texture of plants used as much as possible—for example, an all-white or all-yellow scheme. Another is to pick two colors which contrast strongly with one another, such as orange and blue, purple and yellow, or cerise-pink and lime green. The color-scheme chosen for the wall pot illustrates another option, which is to blend related colors and shades.

The reverse "cool" option to the scheme illustrated here would be a combination of blues, purples, silver, white, and lime green. For more information on color scheming, see the "Color Guide" on pages 26–31.

6 *The primroses flower for several weeks if regularly deadheaded and watered. Hyacinths are not so long-lived. Once the flowers have faded, cut off the heads, but keep the leaves intact.*

Reddish-pink
Hyacinthus

Primula "Wanda" Hybrid

Terracotta wall basket with classical-style relief

49

BUCKETS FULL OF BULBS

While it is important to create different plant and color combinations in hanging baskets and wall containers, sometimes it is the choice of container itself that can make a stunning visual statement. These silvery metal pails are a good example. They can either be hung from brackets, or against a wall, or they will stand alone on the ground.

These bright and shiny metal pails make fun containers, especially for children's gardens, and are easily converted to hanging baskets using a length of silver-colored chain. The mixed planting of bulbs is also unusual but works well because of the contrast of form and color between the different types.

A wide variety of potted bulbs, in bud or flower, is now available in garden centers between late winter and early spring. Dwarf varieties are particularly suited to hanging baskets, especially ones like the dwarf, multi-headed daffodils, grape hyacinths (*Muscari*), chionodoxas, scillas, and *Anemone blanda*, all of which flower over a relatively long period.

Once flowering has finished, take the pails off display, remove the faded heads and continue to feed and water, maintaining the foliage to allow the bulbs to build up reserves for flowering the following spring.

As an alternative to bulbs, you could plant a whole collection of these silver metal pails with individual flowers such as polyanthus or hardy primrose hybrids. Pick bright, paintbox colors—red, yellow, blue, and cerise—and make a cheerful welcome for visitors at the front of the house.

1 *Put a layer of gravel or small pieces of broken polystyrene plant trays to provide a drainage layer at the base of these sealed containers.*

2 *Cover the gravel layer with a little soil—use a gritty, free-draining mix if you do not intend to perforate the base of the pail. Remove handles for easy planting.*

4 *This time using muscari for the central planting, make an outer ring of the smaller, blue and white chionodoxas. Cover any exposed roots or bulbs with more potting mix and water carefully to settle the soil. Take care not to overwater.*

3 *Plant the daffodil centerpiece, leaving enough space for the muscari. Then add the grape hyacinth around the edge of the pail.*

5 *Hang the pails at head height to appreciate the flowers at close quarters. If using multiheaded daffodils, such as "Tête à Tête," pick off individual flowers as they fade.*

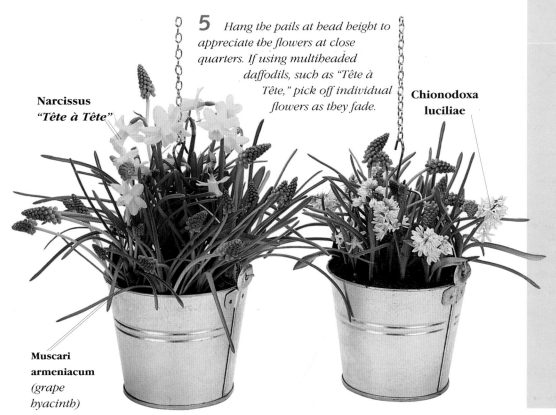

Narcissus "Tête à Tête"

Chionodoxa luciliae

Muscari armeniacum (grape hyacinth)

DIVIDING CLUMPS OF BULBS

Provided you don't damage too many of the roots, individual bulbs can be separated out from their clumps quite safely. Water thoroughly a few hours beforehand.

1 *Gently pull apart the rootball, separating individual bulbs for planting in narrow gaps.*

2 *Tease off some of the soil, reducing the size of the daffodil rootball to fit the pail.*

51

A SPRING WALL BASKET

A large, manger-style basket can create an impressive wall feature to brighten up a bare expanse of brickwork. It could also be used like a windowbox, fixed beneath the frame and enhancing the window above it.

Though it is not very wide, there's room along the length of the manger for a good assortment of plants, and because of the gaps between the bars, you can plant through the front easily. Putting pink and yellow plants next to each other in the garden is normally frowned upon, but this scheme just goes to show how rules about color combinations can often be broken with great success! Using the same types of plant, there are several other colorways which could be tried—for example, for a more vivid scheme try scarlet red tulips like the dwarf "Red Riding Hood," white daisies, deep blue polyanthus, and blue and white violas.

The polyanthus used in this scheme are the exact color of wild primroses, and to take the wild theme a step farther, the spaces between all the plants were filled with moss, giving the impression of a bank in the hedgerow filled with spring flowers.

With the exception of the tulips, the flowers in this basket will keep blooming for weeks provided they have been looked after properly. If the leaves begin to yellow and show signs of starvation, water with a liquid feed. Deadhead regularly and keep a watch for pests.

1 *Line the basket with black plastic. Add a layer of moss high enough to add the first plants.*

2 *Break up bedding strips of violas and feed them through the bars.*

3 *Put three pots of tulips along the back, in as straight a line as possible, allowing room for the other flowers in the foreground.*

4 *Add the yellow polyanthus in a zigzag line, leaving gaps in between for the double daisies.*

5 *Fill in any spaces with double daisies. Add potting mix around the plants and firm them in gently. Cover any gaps with sphagnum moss and water the arrangement thoroughly.*

Bellis perennis

Polyanthus *"Crescendo Primrose"*

Tulipa kaufmanniana *"The First"*

Viola

6 *Once the tulips have started to fade, carefully lift them out intact and plant them in the garden where they can continue to grow and build up reserves for the following year. Replace them with more pot-grown bulbs and spring-flowering herbaceous plants.*

SCHEMES FOR SPRING

Yellow dwarf daffodils, blue *Scilla siberica* or *Muscari* (grape hyacinth), and red primroses with gold-variegated ivy, or variegated *Vinca minor*.

Dark purple tulips, light purple and mauve pink shades of dwarf wallflowers, and silver cineraria with green-leafed *Lamium maculatum*.

Scarlet-red, double-flowered *Ranunculus*, maroon-red *Heuchera* "Palace Purple" and deep red *Dicentra* "Bacchanal" planted with dark green ivy.

White heathers, white polyanthus, white pansy, white *Lamium* "White Nancy."

CAMPANULAS IN SILVER BASKETS

Successful, eye-catching hanging baskets are not always about abundant plantings on a grand scale. Sometimes, small is beautiful. The key to this project is the relative simplicity and straightforwardness of the small-scale planting, combined with containers that are outstandingly attractive in their own right.

Planted up, a pair of these little woven silver baskets would make a lovely gift for a friend or relative. If you prefer a more natural look, there are plenty of tiny wicker baskets to choose from in florists and garden centers. Whatever you choose, for best results, both the planting and method of hanging need to be on the same Lilliputian scale. One basket on its own is unlikely to make sufficient impact, so try two or more baskets hung at different heights, say from a curtain pole across a small window.

In spring, you will often find outdoor plants mixed in with the house plants in garden centers. These are forced into flower early to be used for temporary indoor decoration and may be planted outside once the display has finished. Campanulas and a variety of bulbs make popular subjects for forcing. In this case, an alpine bellflower (*Campanula* sp.), was chosen, its lilac-blue blooms combining beautifully with the silver of the basket. The flowers and leaves are naturally small-scale, but growers can now produce temporarily miniaturized plants which flower at only a few inches tall (see the panel opposite for more mini-flowering plants).

If you like the idea of using dwarf bulbs in baskets, why not pot some up yourself in the fall and grow them on through winter in a cold frame? Once you can see color in the flower buds, plant in baskets, and bring indoors. Try chionodoxa, scilla, crocus, and puschkinia.

1 *It is a good idea to have the baskets to hand when choosing your plants and other materials, such as the ribbon, to see if the combinations will work well.*

Campanula sp.
(alpine bellflower)

2 *To prevent drips, line the basket with a square of transparent plastic. Fold the corners to fit, and trim off any excess at the top.*

3 *Add some gravel or charcoal chippings to provide some drainage, but take care not to overwater, especially drought-tolerant plants.*

MINI BASKET PLANTS

Chrysanthemum
(mini pot mum)
Cyclamen persicum
(mini cyclamen)
Exacum affine
(mini Persian violet)
Kalanchoe blossfeldiana
(mini flaming Katy)
Rosa (mini rose)
Saintpaulia ionantha
(mini African violet)
Houseplant "tots" from garden centers make good foliage plants for small containers.

5 *Hang the baskets in a cool, well-lit position. Suspend using fine florist's ribbon. If the baskets are a gift, you could add some extra ribbon loops and cork screw curls to the handle.*

4 *Plant the campanulas, so that some of the foliage trails over the basket sides. Carefully fill in the gaps between plants with potting mix. Water gently.*

55

A COTTAGE GARDEN BASKET

This wicker basket has a rustic look about it, so the flowers and foliage were chosen to be in keeping with that theme. The planting style is soft and relaxed, just like a traditional cottage garden border.

The hardy alpine bellflower *Campanula carpatica* "Blue Clips" is sometimes brought into flower early by growers and sold as a temporary indoor plant. Here it is teamed up with a gold-leafed, trailing ivy which not only combines well with the blue of the bellflower, but also stands out against the dark colored wicker of the basket.

There are lots of other hardy herbaceous plants and also tender perennials which could be used to give a similar effect, including the dwarf, daisy-flowered marguerites *Argyranthemum frutescens* cultivars) like "Petite Pink," and dwarf scabious, *Scabiosa* "Butterfly Blue" and "Pink Mist," which all flower over a long period. A semi-trailing fuchsia such as the frilly-petalled "Swingtime" would work well in combination with the trailing Verbena "Sissinghurst" or paler pink "Silver Anne."

Many hardy annuals, grown in pots and transferred to the basket when large enough, would also give the required "cottage" look. Try *Nasturtium* "Alaska," with its attractive white-marbled leaves, the citrus pot marigold mix *Calendula* "Fiesta Gitana," or perhaps *Brachyscome iberidifolia* "Summer Skies," which produces a profusion of blue, purple, and white daisies throughout summer. Also, try *Viola* "Watercolors," or "Romeo and Juliet."

1 *Line the basket with black polythene to prevent drips if used indoors, and to protect the wicker. Trim the edge to fit.*

2 *Add some gravel or pieces of broken polystyrene plant trays to create a drainage reservoir which should help prevent over-watering the basket. However, be careful not to put so much drainage material in that you cannot accommodate all your plants!*

3 *For seasonal arrangements indoors and out, use a peat-based potting mix. For border perennials and alpines, use a soil-based mixture or add some coarse grit to the potting mix.*

4 *Plant the variegated ivies to give a rim of greenery to the basket. Arrange the longest trails to spill out over the dipped edge, making the composition asymmetrical.*

5 *Add the campanulas to fill the center of the basket. Try not to completely hide the handle. Fill any gaps with soil and firm.*

With a wide handle like this, use a butcher's hook to suspend the basket from the chain

Campanula carpatica "Blue Clips"

This **Hedera helix** *cultivar (a variegated ivy), combines well with the blue of the bellflower*

6 *Break off chunks of rooted ivy cuttings and use these to fill in any gaps around the edge of the basket.*

7 *Water the basket and hang in a cool, well-lit spot indoors, such as a large glass porch or conservatory.*

JASMINE IN A BLACK WIRE BASKET

There need only to be a few flowers open for you to detect the presence of jasmine.
The perfume is intoxicating, and a single plant in full flower can fill a large room
with fragrance. Jasmine makes a wonderful basket plant because of its
graceful trailing habit and delicate foliage and flower clusters.

*Hang the finished basket in
a well-lit position. Remove
individual flowers as they fade
using a sharp pair of nail
scissors, and water by plunging
the basket in a bucket or
bowl of tepid water.
This will also thoroughly
wet the moss
once again.*

**Jasminum
polyanthum**

The only disadvantage with jasmine is that it is very vigorous and will ultimately need re-planting in a large pot or conservatory border.

You will often see indoor climbers and lax shrubs trained round hoops in garden centers. This is just a way of presenting the plant tidily and is not necessary for its cultivation. Following on from the spring-flowering jasmine, you'll find summer-flowering types like the Passion flower (*Passiflora caerulea*), Cape leadwort (*Plumbago capensis*), *Abutilon* hybrids, and black-eyed Susan (*Thunbergia alata*). All of these can be re-planted to become unusual and eye-catching subjects for hanging baskets. The delicate black-eyed Susan combines well with annuals *(see pg. 96)*, but the others are best planted singly in large baskets, and, like the jasmine, transferred to more conventional containers at the end of the season.

The wirework basket selected for this project was chosen for its elegant lines and emphasizes the romantic feel created by the jasmine's airy trails.

1 *Gently pull out the wire hoop and begin to untangle the stems. This can be a slow and tricky process, but should not be hurried.*

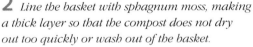

2 *Line the basket with sphagnum moss, making a thick layer so that the compost does not dry out too quickly or wash out of the basket.*

3 *Add a little compost to the fully lined basket. A special hanging basket mix would be ideal. Plant, filling in the sides with more compost.*

4 *Spread out the trailing stems so that they hang evenly over the basket sides. Then wind one or two of the longest trails around the handle.*

5 *To get stems of the plants to trail down the basket into the desired position, pin them in place using long "pins" made from pieces of bent florist's wire. Be careful not to damage the stems with the wire pins.*

59

PAINTING POTS FOR A WEATHERED LOOK

Nowadays, you can obtain a wide range of plastic, terracotta-effect pots. These have the advantage of being unbreakable, frost-proof, and lightweight.

Some pots are more realistic than others, but all have a rather raw, brand new look about them. Over a period of time, real terracotta weathers and takes on the patina of age. White salt deposits work through to the surface and in damp, shady conditions, a coating of green algae often appears. Using a variety of simple paint techniques, it is possible to mimic this transformation and achieve a realistic effect on

plastic containers. Pots and planters with a high relief are the most convincing when painted, as the contours are emphasized by the resultant dark and light shading.

Acrylic paint, mixed and thinned with water, is an ideal medium for this technique, as it remains wet and soluble for long enough to work on and correct any mistakes, but then dries to form a waterproof plastic coating.

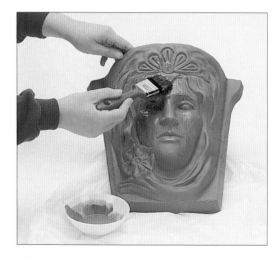

1 *Mix up white, yellow, and dark green artist's acrylic paints, adding water. Apply the first coat.*

2 *Cover the face with a liberal quantity of paint. Do not be too particular at this stage.*

3 *Wipe off excess paint with a piece of absorbent kitchen towel.*

4 *Once dry, apply a second coat. Adjust the mix if the first coat was too dark or light.*

5 *The paint runs down in streaks, giving the effect of weathering and the illusion of age.*

6 *Sponge on some dark green paint to enhance the effect.*

Plecostachys serpyllifolia

Argyranthemum frutescens (*marguerite*)

7 *When the head is dry, plant it up with flowers and foliage to enhance the weathered face. Soft, old-fashioned, and "neutral" colors work well.*

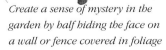

Create a sense of mystery in the garden by half hiding the face on a wall or fence covered in foliage

A Character Wall Pot with Ivy Hair

A wall pot decorated with a carved face adds a touch of theater to the garden.
This project is entitled "The Green Knight," after the figure from Arthurian legend.

1 *Ivy is most often used as a foil for flowers, but in this basket, we have made a feature of the different kinds, blending plain and variegated types.*

The Green Knight's ancient craggy face and untamed beard merely needed some wild locks to frame it, and what better plant to choose for the job than trailing ivy? A mixture of plain-leaved and variegated types gives the effect of silver-streaked hair. Other alternatives for "hair" include the evergreen grasses, for example the blue-leaved fescues (*Festuca*), grass-like plants such as *Carex* species and varieties like "Snowline" and "Evergold." Whatever you use, keep the planting of such pots as simple as possible to highlight rather than compete with the decoration.

Double the dramatic effect by using two identical pots on either side of a doorway or, for a classical look, try mounting a single head at the top of a trellis "pillar" to provide a focus for a bare piece of wall.

Wall pots are often made from terracotta or cast cement which looks like carved stone. They are usually quite small, with room for only a few plants, and because of the limited soil volume, plants tend to dry out quickly. Try to pick as large a container as possible and line unglazed terracotta with plastic to prevent excessive water loss through the sides. Choose plants that will withstand occasional drying out—succulents and silver-leaved plants are ideal for pots attached to a hot, sunny wall.

"Adam"

"Meta"

"Golden Esther"

"Mini Heron"

"Sagittifolia Variegata"

"Goldchild"

2 *Instead of drilling holes, fill the narrow space in the bottom section of the basket with gravel to provide drainage.*

3 *Cover the gravel with potting mixture, filling the wall pot but allowing space on top for the ivies. Try one of the ivies for size.*

4 *Squeeze the rootballs tightly so that you can plant as many different kinds of ivy as possible.*

5 *Remember the basket will be hung against a wall, so arrange some plants so that they stick up at the back.*

IVIES IN WINTER

Ivies are pretty tough customers, but the more heavily variegated an ivy is, the less hardy it is. In cold weather, bring the pot temporarily under cover, or stick to plain-leaved varieties.

Arrange ivy trails against the wall like wisps of unruly hair

This plastic pot has been painted to look like weathered terracotta. (See page 60.)

6 *Fill gaps between the plants with soil and water. Hang the pot in a sheltered, shady position to prevent scorching by winds and sunlight.*

PLANTING UP FOR SUMMER

The sooner you can plant up your summer baskets, the sooner they will start flowering. Baskets kept under glass until they are well established not only look better when hung outdoors, they also tend to be more resilient and less likely to suffer in unfavorable conditions.

If you have a frost-free greenhouse, or conservatory, you could start planting in early spring. Remember, though, that in cold areas prone to late frosts, you may have to keep baskets under cover until early summer.

There is no shortage of basket plants at the very start of the season. Garden centers now sell a wide range of seedlings and rooted cuttings in small pots or "plugs." Some of these are perforated, allowing the roots to grow through the sides, and are designed to be planted pot-and-all to lessen the shock of transplanting. These young plants are sold under various trade names, but are commonly referred to at most garden centers as "tots."

Tots make planting up the sides of baskets a relatively simple affair, and unlike "strip" bedding, where small chunks are separated off, plants suffer little or no root damage. Try to obtain tots for the edges of baskets whenever you need to fill spaces.

1 *Assemble a mixture of flowering and foliage plants.*

2 *Cut out a circle of black plastic and place it in the bottom of the basket, secured with potting mixture. This holds water and prevents soil loss.*

3 *Tuck a layer of sphagnum moss under the edge of the plastic to help disguise it. The plants will finish the job.*

4 *Build up the basket sides with a thick layer of moist sphagnum moss. Add more potting mix.*

5 *Gently push the plugs or rootballs of the rooted cuttings through the basket sides.*

6 *Plant the large ivy, holding the rootball horizontally and feeding the long trails through.*

7 *When the basket sides are planted up, add enough compost to cover all the exposed rootballs.*

8 *Fill the center with upright plants, leaving room for proper development.*

9 *Cover the surface with a thick layer of moss, water, and hang in a light, frost-free place until the plants are established and are growing strongly.*

Fuchsia "La Campanella" *(cascade variety)*

Fuchsia "Beacon" *(bush variety)*

Verbena "Blue Cascade"

Brachyscome multifida

Hedera helix *(variegated ivy)*

Glechoma hederacea "Variegata"

10 *Once young plants develop a good root system, they quickly fill out the basket. Feed them regularly to keep them flowering.*

A SHALLOW BASKET

Baskets are traditionally used for collecting cut flowers, fruit, and vegetables from the garden. They come in all shapes, sizes, and materials, but the basket in this scheme is particularly attractive, with thin strips of curved wood held together by a bamboo frame, adding an oriental touch.

1 *As this is a ready-lined container, you will need to add some gravel or similar material to provide drainage. Expanded clay pellets are also suitable.*

Use peat-based multipurpose or houseplant potting mixture.

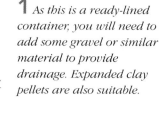

2 *Add a layer of potting mixture. As with all types of container planting, ensure that the plants have been given a thorough soaking beforehand. Try the largest plant in the basket for size to gauge the depth of the compost required.*

To complement the pale, neutral shade of this basket, a scheme of clear, rich colors was chosen, with lacquer-red picking up on the oriental theme.

New Guinea Hybrid *Impatiens* are like giant-flowered versions of the ordinary busy Lizzie. The flower colors are vibrant and the long tapering leaves are either green, bronze, or brightly variegated. There are now many types to choose from and all make superb, long-lasting additions to indoor displays. To keep plants compact and bushy, they need a little more light than bedding *Impatiens*, which can be grown in full shade, though they must be kept out of direct sunlight. They can be grown outdoors in summer, but perform best in a relatively warm, sheltered, and humid environment.

The creeping fig (*Ficus pumila*) thrives in similar conditions and its small, heart-shaped leaves and trailing habit make it a good partner for the *Impatiens*. The tropical red flowers glow all the more surrounded by pure greenery; there is a white-variegated version, but the leaves are very bright and would tend to compete for attention in a scheme like this.

3 *Place the first of the two* Impatiens *in the basket, turning it so that the stems fit round the handle. If the basket is to be viewed from one side only, you can tilt the plant that way.*

4 *Put the other* Impatiens *in to fill the middle portion of the basket. Planting off-center with some stems overhanging, gives the basket a more natural feel.*

5 *Lift the foliage up so that you can fit the creeping figs in underneath. Fill in the gaps round the rootballs with compost as you add in more plants.*

6 *Squeeze in as many of these "filler" plants as you can to create a really lush effect and arrange so that the trails look as though they are growing out between the* Impatiens.

Ficus pumila
(creeping fig)

Impatiens "New Guinea Hybrid"

7 *Hang the finished basket up using natural colored rope or twine to blend with the basket.*

67

RED GERANIUMS IN A WIREWORK WALL BASKET

Wirework baskets offer a stylish alternative to those made of cheaper materials and are worth the extra expense when planted up imaginatively.

Romantic Edwardian-style wirework is back in fashion, and you can now buy quite a wide range of elegant designs to decorate the garden.

The plants in this scheme were chosen to match the delicate framework. Ordinary zonal geraniums would have been too heavy-looking, with their solid flowerheads and large, rounded leaves. Ivy-leafed geraniums are far better suited, the wiry stems covered in attractive foliage creating a much more open and airy effect.

Bearing in mind that most baskets are viewed from below, some foliage or flower detail in the sides of the basket is essential. The brightly variegated kingfisher daisy is a good choice here, as it enjoys the same conditions as the geraniums and never gets too vigorous. Sky blue daisies sometimes appear later in the season, and these would perfectly complement the rich crimson-red geranium flowers.

Other suitable plants for this style of basket include tender perennials like the lilac-blue flowered *Brachyscome multifida*

with feathery foliage and a profusion of daisy flowers, *Argyranthemum* "Petite Pink," a delicate dwarf marguerite with shell-pink blooms, and single fuchsias, such as the red-flowered cascade variety "Marinka."

Above: *Wirework baskets tend to be more expensive than other types, so you will want to show off at least some of the intricate design!*

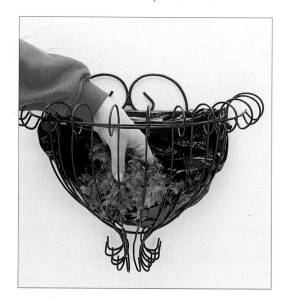

1 *Line the basket with black plastic. Using thick clumps of moist sphagnum moss, begin lining the front of the basket. Tuck some in between the wire and the plastic for camouflage.*

2 *Firm the moss down thoroughly, then add potting mixture up to the point where you intend to plant through the front of the basket.*

3 *Feed the shoots of the kingfisher daisies between the wires. Fill around the plants with more moss, keeping the necks well covered.*

4 *Add the first of the trailing geraniums, arranging the stems so that they point out to the side.*

Ivy-leaved geranium "Barock"

5 *Finish planting the top of the basket, making a balanced arrangement overall that is wider and more fulsome at the top of the basket than at its base.*

6 *Fill in any gaps with soil and water thoroughly. Hang the basket on a sunny wall.*

Deadhead flowers as soon as they start to fade

Variegated **Felicia amelloides**

69

A SUMMER BASKET WITH A PURPLE THEME

Summer is when hanging baskets are at their most colorful and abundant. Why not try something a little different, though, with this unusual purple-themed combination?

1 *Line the basket with black plastic, to act as a water reservoir. Fill the dish of plastic with moist, soilless potting mixture. Even when the top part of the basket is dry, the plant roots should be able to find moisture here.*

2 *Using thick clumps of moist sphagnum moss, begin to line the sides of the basket, tucking the moss under the edges of the plastic to camouflage it.*

3 *Build up the front of the basket with bedding violas pushed horizontally through the bars. Pack in as many as will fit to give a really full display.*

This basket contains an unusual mixture of plants in subtle shades of purple and silver-gray. The deep velvet-purple bedding viola "Prince Henry" makes a wonderful contrast with the other flowers and foliage, and is just right for covering the basket sides. In the top are the daisy-like flowers of *Osteospermum* "Sunny Lady," the deepest color in the Sunny series. Like all osteospermums, the flowers close in shade, so the basket is best hung where it will receive sun for most of the day.

Nemesia caerulea is relatively new on the scene and, perhaps surprisingly, in view of the more familiar nemesias' intolerance of drought, is marketed as a basket and container plant. Airy flower sprays are produced until the frost in a number of pastel shades according to variety.

The foliage in this basket ranges from the fine feathery leaves of *Lotus berthelottii* to the cut leaves of cineraria and rounded, leathery, purple foliage of *Sedum* "Bertram Anderson." The latter can be purchased from the herbaceous perennials section of a garden center.

4 *Fill any gaps between the plants with moss. Next add a group of cineraria, tilting one down over the basket sides to soften the edge. Pinch out the tips of these plants to keep them bushy.*

5 *Plant the large sedum to one side so that its long trailing shoots hang over the edge. In mid-to late summer it produces crimson-red flowers which contrast well with the purple foliage.*

6 *Plant the nemesias to give height at the back of the basket, then add the lotus at the front where it will trail over the edge.*

7 *Fill in the remaining space at the back with the osteospermum, then add more potting mix to cover all exposed rootballs. Water thoroughly.*

8 *To aid moisture retention, cover the potting mix in the top of the basket with a thick layer of moist sphagnum moss.*

Osteospermum *"Sunny Lady"*

Nemesia caerulea

Sedum *"Bertram Anderson"*

Lotus berthelotii *(parrot's beak)*

Viola *"Prince Henry"*

Senecio cineraria *(cineraria)*

71

HOSTAS IN A WOODLAND BASKET FOR A SHADY PLACE

There is no reason why plants from any category, be it alpine, shrub, herbaceous, or houseplant, cannot be used temporarily in a hanging basket, provided it is the right size with an attractive habit and long-lasting color.

With the exception of the variegated ivy, all the plants in this basket were bought from the herbaceous perennials section of a garden center. More drought-tolerant types are obviously better suited, as it is very difficult to keep any basket constantly moist.

There are a number of flowering bedding plants which thrive in shade, including several well-known types like *Fuchsia*, *Impatiens*, *Lobelia* and *Begonia*.

Team them up with ivies or gold-leafed foliage plants like the feathery, golden feverfew (*Tanacetum parthenium* "Aureum"), golden creeping Jenny (*Lysimachia nummularia* "Aurea") or the gold-leafed hosta pictured. Silvers and gray-leafed plants do not normally tolerate shade, which is why the silver-leafed lamiums, including "White Nancy" and the pale rose-flowered "Pink Pewter" illustrated make such useful basket plants.

Although they are more often associated with woodland gardening, some of the fern-like dicentras also work well in shady environments. Here, the blue-gray leaved variety "Pear Drops" makes a wonderful contrast with the golden hosta.

2 *Pour in some moisture-retentive potting mix. The thick liner will also protect the plants from drying out.*

1 *There are various options for lining hanging baskets, many of which use re-cycled or waste materials such as this coir matting. (See page 16.)*

Stand the basket in the top of a large flower pot to keep it stable while you work

3 *Plant the dicentra, as with all plants, leaving enough of a gap at the top to allow for thorough watering.*

72

4 *Next add the gold-leafed hosta variety "August Moon.". As well as having strikingly architectural foliage, it also produces spikes of very pale pink bellflowers in midsummer.*

5 *Plant the ground covering lamium in the remaining third of the basket. This variety produces a profusion of pink-hooded flowers throughout midsummer.*

6 *The lamium will grow out, but for instant trails, add rooted cuttings of a gold-variegated* Hedera helix *variety.*

8 *Hang the basket in a sheltered shaded site. At the end of the season, you could transfer the plants to the garden. Alternatively, why not plant them together in a wooden half barrel with some dwarf spring bulbs for a woodland effect?*

Dicentra *"Pearl Drops"* has blue-gray foliage

Hosta *"August Moon"*

7 *When the basket is full of plants, fill in any gaps with potting mix, then add a thick layer of moist sphagnum moss or fine chipped bark to act as a mulch.*

Hedra helix *cultivar (ivy)*

Lamium maculatum *"Pink Pewter,"* *a pale rose-flowered variety.*

A PINK BASKET FOR COOL SHADE

Busy Lizzies (*Impatiens*) are invaluable for baskets as they come in such a wide range of colors from almost fluorescent reds, pinks, and purples, through to soft pastel shades and white. You can also get varieties with white striped petals, pale varieties with darker "eyes", or picotee types like the one illustrated with darker edged petals.

Single F1 hybrid bedding varieties of *Impatiens* tend to give the best performance outdoors. You can get pretty doubles too, but these tend to be less resistant to poor weather conditions. Busy Lizzies thrive in shade but will also grow happily in full sun, though some darker-flowered varieties can bleach unless given a shaded aspect.

Color matching impatiens with other plants is easy because of the choice of single colors now available from garden centers. Here a soft pink shade has been selected to highlight the pink splashed leaves of the variegated *Tradescantia*. Try teaming up white-variegated apple mint or spider plants (*Chlorophytum*) with pure white *Impatiens* or, for a more vibrant alternative, match orange, cerise pink, or red *Impatiens* with the variegation on *Solenostemon* (coleus) leaves.

The trailing forms of *Tradescantia* are amongst the most popular of all house plants, probably because they are so easy to grow and propagate. Cuttings root in water in a matter of days, after which several

3 *Plant the basket sides using bedding impatiens with small rootballs.*

1 *Line the back and base of the basket with black plastic. Add a layer of sphagnum moss.*

2 *Line with moss near to the top. Fill the base with a recommended mixture for baskets.*

4 *Surround the necks of the plants with more sphagnum moss.*

cuttings should then be planted in the same pot to give a fuller effect early on. Several forms are available, including white-, pink-, and purple-variegated types as well as plain-leafed varieties. Outdoors, grow them in sun or moderate shade, but avoid deep shade, as this tends to cause variegated forms to revert to all-green.

There are several other house and conservatory plants which will perform well in outdoor baskets through the summer months *(see Panel)*. If you start propagating in early spring, you can have lots of strong young plants ready for hardening off and planting in early summer. Alternatively buy houseplant "tots" and pot them on to promote rapid growth prior to planting.

5 *Add the tradescantias until the basket is full. Leave a gap at the back and plant extra impatiens that will grow taller.*

HOUSEPLANTS OUTSIDE

Abutilon megapotamicum "Variegatum"
Asparagus densiflorus Sprengeri Group
Asparagus setaceus (syn. *A. plumosus*)
Begonia sutherlandii
Ceropegia woodii
Chlorophytum comosum "Variegatum"
Kalanchoe blossfeldiana
Saxifraga stolonifera
Scirpus cernuus
Soleirolia soleirolii (formerly *Helxine*)
Solenostemon (coleus)
Tolmiea menziesii "Taff's Gold"
Tradescantia zebrina

Tradescantia fluminensis "Tricolor"

Impatiens "Super Elfin Swirl" *F1* (busy Lizzie)

6 *Fill in any gaps with soil and water thoroughly. Hang on a shady, sheltered wall.*

75

THYME, SAGE AND VERBENA

Variegated and colored-leafed herbs make attractive additions to baskets and wall planters. They often perform better than more conventional basket plants in hot, dry summers, thriving in the well-drained conditions and not minding the occasional missed watering.

As well as looking good, variegated and colored-leafed herbs also smell good. Hang them within easy reach so that people can gently rub the foliage and release the aromatic oils.

In general, variegated herbs are not as strongly flavored as plain-leafed species, but their foliage is useful for garnishing various dishes and drinks. If growing herbs in a basket for the kitchen, you could plant a combination of good

2 *To ensure that the hole at the bottom does not clog up with potting mix, add a layer of gravel.*

3 *Use a peat-based multi-purpose potting mix.*

1 *Terracotta wall pots in sunny positions lose moisture rapidly, so always line with plastic before planting. This will hold in water at the bottom of the pot and will assist the growing medium in retaining moisture up the sides of the pot. Ensure that the plastic fits comfortably to the very top of the wall pot. Cut a hole in the bottom of the plastic to allow for drainage.*

4 *Plant the lemon thyme in the center of the wall pot. Then add a variegated sage to one side.*

5 *Plant a white-flowered trailing or upright verbena in the center and then another variegated sage to match the one on the opposite side. Deep cerise pink, scarlet, purple, or golden-yellow flowers work equally well.*

6 *Fill in the gaps at each end with more verbenas. Most trailing types will need cutting back now and then to keep them under control. This may not be necessary with the blue-purple, cascade variety which has more delicate foliage.*

SPRING BASKET

At the end of summer, dismantle the basket, removing the salvias and verbenas. You could leave the thyme in position and fill the space behind with crocus bulbs, such as *Crocus chrysanthus* "Cream beauty," or "Zwanenburg Bronze." Pack the bulbs in tightly for a good display in early spring.

culinary types along with more decorative varieties and add a few edible flowers like nasturtium, *Calendula* (pot marigold), and viola for extra color.

Herbs add significantly to the range of foliage plants that you can use in baskets. For baskets in full sun, try sages such as the all-purple *Salvia officinalis* "Purpurascens," the pretty pink, white, and purple variegated *S.o.* "Tricolor," or the yellow variegated *S.o.* "Icterina" illustrated here. Creeping thymes are useful year-round for covering the sides of baskets—plant bushier, more upright types in the top of your baskets for the best effects. There are many golden and variegated varieties to choose from and you will find them in both the herb and alpine sections of most garden centers. For baskets in shade, you could try using one of the variegated mints, golden marjoram, or the feathery-leafed, golden feverfew.

Verbena *"Sissinghurst White"*

Salvia officinalis *"Icterina"*

Thymus × citriodorus *"Aureus"*

7 *Hang on a wall which is in sun for at least half the day. Feed and water regularly. Keep a watch for powdery mildew on the verbenas and if necessary spray with a systemic fungicide.*

A SUMMER DISPLAY IN A MANGER BASKET

This scheme shows how easy it is to give the same container a whole new look simply by choosing very different plants to fill it (see page 52 for alternative spring schemes).

Large containers like these give far greater scope for combining plants creatively— generally speaking, the bigger the container, the more types of flower and foliage can be used, especially when fairly tight color schemes are being planned.

When choosing plants for a container, it pays to imagine what size and shape they will develop into after several weeks of growth. That way you will avoid situations where one plant becomes out of proportion with the rest. This is not always easy to achieve, since information on the plant label can often be rather sketchy and most young plants are of a similar size when you buy them. You will sometimes need to trim back individual plants, and it is better to begin to control vigorous types early on. For example, in the scheme featured here, the silver-leaved cinerarias will need occasional pinching out to keep them bushy and in their best shape, as well as the removal of over-large leaves or shoots in the weeks ahead.

1 *Line the back and base of the basket with black plastic. Then line the front of the basket with sphagnum moss, tucking it under the plastic.*

2 *Pour some potting mix into the base of the basket and then insert the first row of widely spaced* Ageratum *plants.*

3 *Build up the front of the basket with pink* Impatiens *and more* Ageratum, *varying the height of the plants so that the arrangement looks more natural.*

4 *To stabilize plants and prevent the rootballs from drying out, pack in plenty of moist moss.*

5 *Plant three zonal geraniums at the back. Look for plants labelled C.V.I. (Culture Virus Indexed).*

6 *Plant a row of cut-leafed cineraria at the front to provide strong textural contrast. Tilt them forward to cover the basket edge.*

7 *Add F1 hybrid petunias between the geraniums and cineraria. These floribunda types are compact, free-flowering, and weather resistant.*

Senecio cineraria *(cineraria)*

Petunia *F1 Hybrid* "Mirage Series"

Pelargonium *F1 Hybrid* "PAC Fox"

Ageratum *F1 Hybrid* "Blue Danube"

Impatiens *F1 hybrid* "Novette Series"

8 *Work potting mix into all the gaps and cover the entire surface of the basket with a thick layer of sphagnum moss. Water thoroughly and then hook the basket onto a sunny wall with two large protruding screws.*

A Classic White Arrangement

The famous white garden at Sissinghurst Castle in Kent has been emulated by many people seeking to create the same feeling of tranquillity and purity in their own gardens. There is something about the way in which white, gray, silver, and green foliage combine that is so restful to the eye.

For any monochrome scheme to be truly successful though, it is important to have plenty of textural contrast between the different elements. Here, the large, solid flower heads of petunia are planted beside the smaller-flowered busy Lizzie and the busy Lizzie is in turn set against the froth of white alyssum. Foliage is no less important. The ferny, gray-leafed lotus has a totally different feel to the trailing ivy and both make a good contrast with the large, rounded leaves of the geranium.

When you select plants for a white-schemed basket, you will realize that there is a noticeable variation in the color of white flowers. Those in the basket are pure white and work well together, but the results may not have been so successful if, say, both creamy whites and pure whites had been used.

Apart from the plants mentioned above, there are several other good white-variegated basket plants to choose from including the aromatic and drought-resistant *Plectranthus coleoides* "Marginatus," the familiar trailing nepeta or variegated ground ivy (*Glechoma hederacea* "Variegata"), and the variegated succulent trailer, *Sedum lineare* "Variegatum."

1 *Cut a circle of plastic and place it in the base of the basket. Fill with potting mix.*

2 *The plastic traps water in the base. Camouflage it with moss.*

3 *Cover the basket sides with sweet-smelling white alyssum, feeding the rootballs through the wrought-iron sides of the basket.*

4 *Plant the busy Lizzie, angling the plant so that it covers the rim as far as possible.*

5 *Plant a pot of* Lotus berthelotii *to trail over the edge. Next begin planting petunias.*

6 *Build up the sides with moss. Next add a trailing ivy.*

Pelargonium "Aphrodite" *(a PAC cultivar)*

Impatiens *(busy Lizzie)*

Lotus berthelotii *(parrot's beak)*

Petunia "Celebrity White"

7 *Squeeze a white-flowered geranium into the space remaining in the center of the basket. Fill remaining gaps with soil and water copiously. It is especially important to fill remaining gaps carefully with soil to avoid air pockets which could allow the rootballs to dry out.*

Lobularia maritima "Snow Crystals" *(sweet white alyssum)*

Hedera helix *(variegated ivy)*

8 *Replace the chains and hang in a sunny position where the smell of the alyssum can be appreciated.*

81

A ROMANTIC HANGING BASKET

Tissue-paper begonias and airy asparagus fern combine to give this wall basket the feel of a bouquet of flowers, and the rose-pink color scheme adds to the air of romance. This is a basket for a site sheltered from wind and the bleaching effect of strong sunlight, where the luxuriant foliage and flowers can continue to grow unscathed.

Large-leafed tuberous begonias are normally sold singly, in flower, making it easy to choose just the right shade. The F1 Hybrid "Non-Stop" variety is always a good choice and is widely available.

Since hanging baskets are nearly always attached to the walls of a house, it follows that schemes are best chosen to blend with or emphasize the architecture around them. This basket would work well on an elegant Victorian or Edwardian-style building, but might look out of place on the walls of an ultra-modern town house.

Schemes can be chosen to pick up colors used on and around the house and garden, such as the color of a front door, garden gate, or trellis. Orange-red brickwork can make a difficult backdrop for baskets, especially those containing pink flowers. Although the "safe" answer is to pick schemes containing "neutral" silvers, grays and white, blues and purples, baskets can be even more eye-catching planted predominantly with flame reds and oranges, and touches of cream, or golden-yellow flowers, and bronze-purple, blue-gray, and silver foliage.

1 *Line the back of the basket with black plastic cut from an old potting mix bag.*

2 *Line the front with a thick layer of moist sphagnum moss.*

3 *Turning the pot on its side, feed the stems of the lamium through the bars to cover the front.*

4 *Add potting mix to support and cover the rootball.*

5 *Split up a tray of bedding begonias and feed plants through between the bars to fill in around the lamium stems.*

6 *Add an asparagus fern (previously hardened off outdoors,) leaving a gap at the front for more bedding begonias.*

7 *Fill in any spaces in the basket with more bedding begonias and soil.*

**Begonia ×
tuberhybrida**

**Asparagus
setaceus**
*(asparagus fern)
—not a fern at
all, but a relative
of the lily.*

**Lamium maculatum
"Pink Pearls"**
*(deadnettle)—
a hardy herbaceous
ground cover plant*

**Begonia ×
tuberhybrida**

**Begonia
semperflorens
"Olympia Pink" F1**
*(fibrous-rooted or
bedding begonia)*

8 *Water the basket well and do not allow it to dry out. Overwinter the fleshy begonia tubers in a frost-free place and bring the asparagus fern indoors.*

83

A WALL BASKET OF PORTULACUS FOR A HOT SUNNY SPOT

Vibrantly colored portulacas are the perfect choice for this little Mexican-style glazed wall pot, which is excellent for a south-facing wall.

These succulents thrive in a sun-baked position. In shade or if the sun goes in, they close up their flowers. Other sun worshipers which behave in the same way are the daisy-flowered osteospermums, gazanias, arctotis, and the Livingstone daisy (*Dorotheanthus bellidiformis* syn. *Mesembryanthemum criniflorum*). The latter would be a good substitute for the portulacas, with its drought-resistant, fleshy leaves, and low, trailing habit.

Portulacas tend to be sold during mid-summer as mature plants already in flower. Pots often contain a blend of different shades, which gives a very rich effect. The flowers are grouped in tight clusters at the shoot tips. It is quite difficult to remove spent flowers individually without damaging the buds, so wait until the whole cluster has flowered and then cut the stem back to a side shoot. Be careful not to overwater succulent plants like these—it is better to let them dry out slightly between waterings. For this reason, if you want to mix portulacas with other foliage, choose similarly drought-resistant types, including helichrysum, *Senecio cineraria*, geraniums, sedum, and sempervivum.

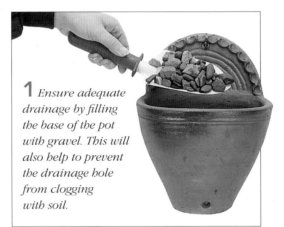

1 *Ensure adequate drainage by filling the base of the pot with gravel. This will also help to prevent the drainage hole from clogging with soil.*

2 *Use a soil-based potting mix with extra grit if necessary—peat-based types do not drain as freely and if they dry out, are very difficult to re-wet.*

FITTING IN PLANTS

If you squeeze the root-ball of a pot-grown plant out of its circular shape into a flattened oval, you can pack more plants into the same space and thereby achieve a greater concentration of color.

3 *Try the first plant in the pot. When planting, tilt the rootball slightly so that the arching stems hang over the side of the pot.*

4 *Add the central plant, again tilting it so that the stems hang down over the front of the pot. Leave room at the back for another plant.*

Portulaca grandiflora

Always ensure that wall pots like this have adequate drainage, especially when glazed, as excess moisture cannot escape through the sides as it does in plain terracotta

5 *Balance the shape of the basket by adding a third plant on the left hand side.*

6 *Add the final plant in the space at the back of the pot and fill any remaining gaps with soil. Hang the pot where it will receive sunshine for most of the day.*

GRASS AND SUCCULENTS IN A TERRACOTTA WALL POT

This simply decorated, terracotta wall pot has a strong Mediterranean feel, with sun-loving succulents, and the steely-blue grass *Festuca glauca*.

1 *Cover the hole in the base with a stone to prevent soil escaping. Do not block the hole so thoroughly that water cannot drain out.*

2 *Fill the base with a soil-based potting mixture. Check the depth as usual. You need to ensure that you put enough growing medium in while leaving sufficient room for the plants.*

3 *The blue-leaved fescues provide excellent foliage contrast in baskets. They combine especially well with brilliantly colored flowers— yellows, oranges, and hot reds.*

Planting schemes invariably work best when the flowers and foliage are chosen to complement the container, and this is a good example of that rule. There are many different varieties of *Sempervivum* (house leek), with fleshy rosettes in various colors, from almost white to dark purple-red. They wouldn't normally be considered for basket planting, but at the front of a small pot like this, their architectural form can be properly appreciated. An alternative group of succulents with similar looks are the frost tender echeverias. *Echeveria secunda* var. *glauca* has beautiful, pale blue-gray leaves and contrasting spikes of yellow and red. Look for it in the houseplant section of your garden center.

Flaming Katy (kalanchoe) is another house plant which, once hardened off, is perfectly happy outdoors during the summer months.

4 *Plant the house leek at the front of the pot and tilt it slightly so that you can see the rosette more clearly.*

5 *Plant the first of the kalanchoes at the back of the basket, filling in the space between the grass and houseleek with extra soil.*

Sempervivum "Feldmaier" (house leek)

Festuca glauca (fescue)

6 *Add the remaining kalanchoe, tilting it out to the side slightly to balance the shape of the basket. Alternatively, use the succulent trailer Sedum lineare "Variegatum."*

7 *Hook the wall pot onto two screws fixed in a bright position but out of strong midday sun, otherwise the kalanchoe flowers fade too rapidly.*

Kalanchoe blossfeldiana (flaming Katy)

A CASCADE OF WHITE AND GOLD

The dark green of this plastic wall trough makes an excellent foil for the
bright, lime-coloured trails of creeping Jenny and the bushy spiraea in the center.
Overall, the color scheming is quite subtle, but on a white wall,
the result is cool, leafy luxuriance.

The delicate white-flowered trailer, formerly sold under the name *Bacopa*, is set to become an immensely popular basket and container plant. Its correct name is *Sutera cordata* "Snowflake." Because of its compact growth and profusion of tiny white flowers, it is an excellent "filler" for baskets, but it also makes a stunning display when planted all on its own, its stems growing down to cover the basket sides completely.

Trough-like wall baskets lend themselves to symmetrical planting. In a relatively short basket like this you really only need one specimen plant as a centerpiece. The pinky-red flowers of the spiraea provide quite a long display, but it is the bright leaf color contrasting with the bronze-tinted new growth which is the main attraction. If you keep it well fed and watered, this basket will continue to look fresh right through into the fall.

Take cuttings of *Sutera* before the frosts to ensure a supply for next year and plant out the hardy lysimachia and spiraea in the garden. Both of these prefer a slightly shaded spot to prevent leaf scorch.

1 *Puncture the base of the trough for drainage—the spots are normally marked on for you. Add gravel to provide extra drainage.*

2 *Put in a quantity of multi-purpose potting mix. Check the level with the largest plant.*

3 *Soak the rootball. Place the spiraea in the center of the trough.*

4 *Next add pots of the gold-leaved creeping Jenny.*

TRAILING PLANTS

Begonia × tuberhybrida varieties

Bidens ferulifolia

Convolvulus sabatius

Fuchsia (trailing varieties)

Geranium (ivy-leaved varieties, especially "Balcon," "Decora," "Cascade" and "Mini-Cascade" types)

Glechoma hederacea "Variegata" (variegated ground ivy)

Hedera helix varieties

Helichrysum petiolare and varieties e.g. "Limelight," "Variegatum"

Lamium maculatum "White Nancy,"

"Pink Pewter"

Lobelia (trailing varieties, e.g, "Fountain" and "Cascade" series

Lotus berthelotii

Petunia, Surfinia F1 series

Scaevola aemula "Blue Wonder"

Sedum lineare "Variegatum"

Thunbergia alata (black-eyed Susan)

Tropaeolum "Empress of India," "Gleam Hybrids" (nasturtium)

Verbena

Spiraea japonica

Sutera cordata

6 *Provided the basket is fed and watered regularly, it will need little in the way of maintenance. Snip off the dead spiraea heads when the flowering has finished and trim plants to shape if any grows out of proportion.*

Sutera *thrives in sun or part shade and flowers non-stop all summer*

Spiraea japonica "Magic Carpet"

5 *Fill the remaining gaps with* Sutera. *As well as white-flowered plants, the gold foliage in this basket would also look good with blue or purple lobelias, cerise-pink, and red fuchsias, or* Begonia semperflorens.

Lysimachia nummularia "Aurea"

Sutera cordata "Snowflake"

89

A LARGE DISPLAY OF PURPLE AND YELLOW

The daisy-like heads of *Asteriscus maritimus* create a splash of gold at the center of this basket. This recent arrival to the container and patio plants section of garden centers is in fact a rock garden plant.

With its dense spreading habit, attractive round-ended leaves, and profusion of flowers, it makes an excellent basket plant, too.

Another recently established plant is *Verbena* "Homestead Purple," a vigorous native cultivar with wiry stems ending in

There are several different types of liner, often made from recycled waste products. Choose dark-colored liners, as they tend to fade into the background when you plant up the basket

1 *Lay a sheet of recycled wool liner in the basket and press into position, folding the fabric as necessary. Trim off the excess material with a pair of sharp scissors.*

large, vivid, purple flowerheads. It makes a perfect contrast with all the yellow and gold plants in the basket.

In order to camouflage the basket sides, several pots of a yellow variegated ivy with long trails were used. Ivy is an indispensable basket plant. Not only does it come in a bewildering variety of leaf shape and variegation, it is also extremely tough and tolerates a wide range of conditions. Small plants, little more than rooted cuttings at the start of the summer basket season, will have grown into good-sized specimens for instant effect by the time you need them for winter and spring basket planting.

Another plant which could be salvaged from this basket and used as a centerpiece for a winter arrangement is the yellowish-green tree heath, *Erica arborea* "Albert's Gold," whose feathery foliage adds textural interest as well as color. This plant would eventually grow to 6 feet in height if grown in open ground, and needs to be pruned to keep it dense and compact. Provide a well-lit situation to enhance coloring.

2 *Add potting mix. As this is a 16-in basket, use a non-loam based type so that it does not get too heavy.*

3 *Cover the front and sides of the basket with yellow-variegated trailing ivy planted in the top.*

90

Below: Fill in the gaps between plants with more potting mix and water thoroughly. Allow to drain and then hang in a sunny position. Make sure for safety's sake that you use the correct size bracket for this very heavy basket.

4 *Next add some* Asteriscus, *arranging the stems to hang over the ivy and create a ring of flowers. Deadhead as soon as any flowers turn brown.*

5 *Plant a specimen of* Erica arborea *"Albert's Gold" in the center of the basket. Don't worry about soil pH, as* E. arborea *is very flexible.*

6 *Fill the remaining space at the back with the purple-flowered verbena, arranging the stems so that some trail forward and intermingle with the asteriscus flowers. Deadhead to encourage further blooms.*

Erica arborea "Albert's Gold"
(tree heath)

Verbena "Homestead Purple"

Hedera helix cultivar
(variegated ivy)

91

A SUBTROPICAL HANGING BASKET

The brilliant blooms of the Brazilian scarlet sage (*Salvia splendens*) give an exotic, subtropical feel to this basket of lush foliage plants. Foliage is not often considered bold enough to act as much more than a foil for flowers, but here plants like the multi-colored *Houttuynia* and gold-striped sedge take center stage.

Houttuynia is quite an adaptable plant and will grow in the margins of a pond as well as in a damp border or well-watered container. However, if you do plant it in the garden, be warned—its underground runners spread very quickly! The form used in this basket is *H. cordata* "Chameleon." Unlike the plain-leaved form, "Chameleon" needs a well-lit position to develop its coloring properly. During summer, small white flowers with a domed center sometimes appear. Another curious feature is that if you break off a leaf and smell the sap, it is strongly aromatic, very like the aroma of Seville oranges.

The variegated sedge, *Carex oshimensis* "Evergold" is another plant which is easy to please, provided its roots do not run short of water. The stiff, grassy foliage arching over the basket sides contrasts perfectly with the broader-leaved *Houttuynia* and *Salvia*. At the end of summer, when the display is dismantled, save the carex for use in a winter hanging basket or plant at the front of a border in sun or shade to add sparkle to a planting of other winter evergreens. As a

dramatic black-leafed alternative to the sedge, you could use another Japanese plant, the evergreen *Ophiopogon planiscapus* "Nigrescens."

The final element in this basket is a bronze-purple form of bugle, *Ajuga reptans* "Atropurpurea." Bugles are normally evergreen to semi-evergreen, depending on the variety and severity of the winter. For the most reliable purple foliage, suitable for covering the sides of a winter basket, choose the cultivar "Braunherz." Blue flower spikes normally appear in spring, but bonus flowers often develop later in the year as you can see from the photograph. Ajugas dislike very dry conditions and grow more rapidly when watered freely. Transferred to the border, they make excellent low ground cover. Bugles are often sold as rock-garden plants, but are really too invasive for such a situation.

Variations on this subtropical theme can be achieved by using other colorful and interesting variegated plants. These are becoming widely available and increasingly inexpensive at most garden centers.

1 *Cut a circle of black plastic and place it in the bottom of the basket. This will retain water. Camouflage with sphagnum moss.*

2 *Fill the basket with a moisture-retentive potting mix. Build up the sides of the basket with a thick lining of moss.*

3 *Plant three red salvias at the back of the basket. The scarlet bracts remain colorful long after the protruding flowers have faded, but once the main spike has gone over, it can be removed to make way for the shorter flowering side shoots.*

Salvia splendens *variety*
(scarlet sage)

Houttuynia cordata "Chameleon"

Ajuga reptans "Atropurpurea" *(purple-leafed bugle)*

7 *Mulch the top of the basket with a thick layer of sphagnum moss and stand in a sheltered spot out of direct sun for a few days to allow plants to settle in. Afterward, hang in full sun.*

Carex oshimensis "Evergold" *(variegated sedge)*

4 *Add a couple of trailing, purple-leafed bugles to cover one side of the basket. Smaller plants could also be planted between the bars.*

5 *Plant the variegated sedge on the opposite side, leaving sufficient room in the middle for the Houttuynia. Soak the rootball before planting.*

6 *After soaking, add the final plant, tilting it slightly to display the variegated foliage. You may need to squeeze the rootball out of shape to fit it in. Fill any gaps between the plants with potting mixture. Add more soil if necessary to fill spaces.*

93

A LATE-SEASON PASTEL DISPLAY

You can plant virtually anything in a hanging basket: this arrangement uses a mixture of tender bedding plants and hardy shrubs. Baskets are traditionally made up in spring, with planting that will last through the whole of summer, but that restricts the range of plants that you can use and does not allow for any seasonal variation.

Hypericums and hebes are two of the mainstays of the late summer and fall border, and there are compact varieties which also make good temporary subjects for baskets. The low-growing *Hypericum* x *moserianum* "Tricolor" is a good choice for the front, and *Hebe* "Purple Pixie" is just one of a range of small-leafed hebes which flower during summer and fall. For a longer lasting display,

go for varieties like *Hebe* "Autumn Glory" or "Sapphire." Other possible alternatives for the back of the basket include the blue-flowered *Caryopteris* x *clandonensis* or perhaps *Ceratostigma willmottianum*. For fall color at the front, you could use dwarf Michaelmas daisies, heathers (*Calluna* and *Erica* cultivars), or maybe the creeping *Ceratostigma plumbaginoides*.

3 *While planting up just one side of a basket or when adding a single large plant, you may find that the basket tips over, despite the fact it is standing in a heavy pot for stability. To keep it stable and level, counterbalance the weight using a small heavy object, such as a half brick or similarly sized stone.*

1 *Use a self-watering basket for this display. Stand in a heavy plant pot. Add potting mixture.*

2 *Cover the whole base with potting mixture. Offer up the largest plant to check the soil level.*

FITTING A LARGE PLANT INTO A BASKET

When you tip a newly-purchased shrub or herbaceous plant out of its pot, you will often find it contains a lot of loose soil at the base. Before planting, shake or gently tease the excess away from the roots so that you can fit it into the relatively shallow basket.

4 *Arrange the trailing sedum to hang over the right side of the basket and on the opposite side, plant the variegated hypericum. Add in extra sedums to fill in any gaps.*

5 *White* Begonia semperflorens *with their yellow-centered flowers make a visual link between the white-variegated sedum and yellow-flowered hypericum, and bridge the height gap between the front and rear of the basket.*

6 *This combination of gentle colors was chosen to complement the pale, stone-colored basket. Hang in a well-lit spot sheltered from strong midday sun.*

Hebe *"Purple Pixie"*

Hypericum × moserianum *"Tricolor"*

Begonia semperflorens

Sedum lineare *"Variegatum"*

95

DAHLIAS IN A WICKER BASKET

This rustic wicker basket, with its soft orange and bronzey-purple coloring, has a distinctly autumnal feel. It overflows with the charming annual climber, *Thunbergia alata*, commonly known as black-eyed Susan. This is very easy to raise from seed in spring and much less expensive than buying plants in flower during summer.

The stems of black-eyed Susan sometimes get a little congested, so some judicious thinning may be called for to emphasize its elegant trailing habit. Then, match the flower shade exactly with a pot of bedding dahlias. In late summer, garden centers are full of these plants, with their showy blooms in a wide range of rich colors. Bedding dahlias are ideal for container planting.

The glossy bronze-purple foliage of the bugle, *Ajuga reptans* "Atropurpurea" makes a striking contrast with the paler *Thunbergia*, and the trailing foliage rosettes soften the sides of the basket well. The more upright *Euphorbia* provides a lighter texture altogether and makes an attractive "filler." This is a relatively recent introduction named "Chameleon."

1 *Line the basket with black plastic. Fill the base of the basket with moistened peat-based potting mixture. Firm lightly and then offer up the first plant to see if the level is right.*

2 *When using plants that have filled their pots with roots, it is important to soak the rootball before planting it. Submerge it in a bucket and wait until the stream of air bubbles stops.*

3 *Weigh down the opposite side of the basket with something heavy, to stop it tipping over as you plant the dahlia.*

4 *Lift up the dahlia foliage and tuck the* Ajuga *in underneath, arranging the trails so that they fall over the edge of the basket.*

5 *Add a couple of pots of* Euphorbia *in the gap between the dahlia and black-eyed Susan. Take care with this plant, as all euphorbias exude a milky-white irritant sap if damaged.*

Euphorbia dulcis "Chameleon"

Dahlia "Dahlietta Apricot"—*bedding dahlia*

Ajuga reptans "Atropurpurea"

Thunbergia alata (*black-eyed Susan*)

6 *Complete the basket with more ajugas and fill in around plants with potting mix. Hang up in a position out of extreme midday sun, which would bleach the flowers.*

VIOLAS AND IVY WITH A FUCHSIA FOR FOLIAGE

In the border, the beauty of individual flowering plants can often be enhanced with a suitable backdrop of foliage. Here the same principle has been applied to highlight a mass of viola blooms.

Bedding violas come in a range of shades including plain and bicoloured varieties. Some are almost black and tend to "disappear" in a mixed arrangement. This velvet purple variety is much more visible with its paler lilac center, but still needs to be surrounded by lighter foliage to do it justice. White variegated plants complement the flowers perfectly. The elegant fuchsia variety "Sharpitor" used at the back of the basket is quite unlike most bedding varieties. It has very pale green leaves edged creamy white with slender pendant flowers of blush pink which are most profuse in fall. It is frost hardy, so when the display is dismantled, it can be re-planted in the border. Variegated ground ivy and real ivy provide a foil at the front.

1 *Cut a circle of black plastic from an old potting mix bag and use it to line the base of the basket. Camouflage the edges with sphagnum moss.*

2 *The plastic lining traps moisture and acts like a small reservoir for the plants to draw on between waterings. Fill with potting mix and add more moss.*

3 *Separate a pot of rooted ivy cuttings and plant some between the basket wires, packing round the neck with moss to prevent drying out and loss of soil.*

4 *Soak remaining plants before use, then add the fuchsia specimen, positioning it at the back of the basket. Plant the first of the violas, leaving room for the ground ivy.*

5 *Add pots of trailing ground ivy around the edge of the basket to mingle with the ivy trails. Ground ivy roots easily from cuttings, and once you have a plant, you should theoretically never need to buy another!*

Fuchsia magellanica var. molinae "Sharpitor" *(variegated hardy fuchsia)*

Bedding violas

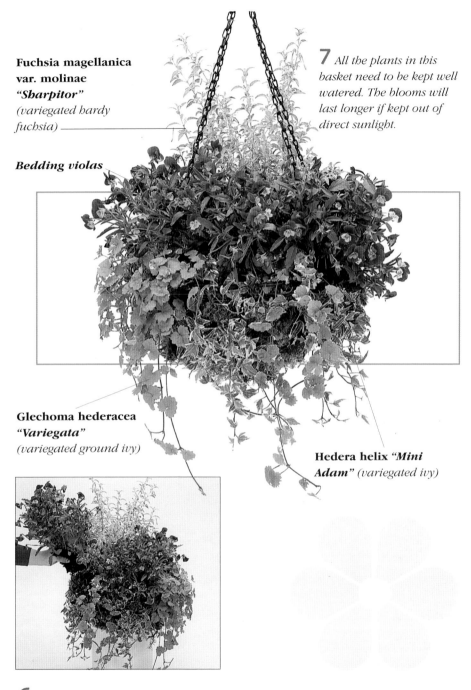

7 *All the plants in this basket need to be kept well watered. The blooms will last longer if kept out of direct sunlight.*

Glechoma hederacea "Variegata" *(variegated ground ivy)*

Hedera helix "Mini Adam" *(variegated ivy)*

6 *Finish planting the violas and fill in any gaps between plants with more potting mixture. The viola flowers will re-orientate themselves over the next few days. Deadhead frequently to keep the blooms coming.*

99

AN IVY CHICKEN BASKET

Planted with moss and ivy, and hung by the front door, this chicken basket is sure to attract attention! Extra-small-leafed ivies are a good choice here, as they make a dense evergreen covering without obscuring the detail of the container.

Hedera helix
"Mini Adam"

This basket demonstrates a simple but very effective technique which can be used to make other hanging shapes, including spheres which are made by joining two ordinary wire hanging baskets together.

You can either plant in the top of the basket and train foliage to cover the outside as shown here or, using small, rooted cuttings, plant directly through the sides. Baskets made in this way are more tricky to keep, especially during very hot weather, as you really need to keep the moss moist to keep it green in the exposed extremities. The easiest method is to soak the basket by sitting the base in a bowl of water. The sphagnum moss acts like a wick and draws water up through the shape. You should also add water as normal in the top of the basket to ensure that the potting mixture remains moist at all times. If grown indoors or in a conservatory, mist spray daily.

This is really a form of framed topiary and will need a certain amount of trimming and training to keep the figure in shape. Take care to keep the features of the head clear of foliage, as they would easily be obscured.

1 *This unusual wire basket is actually an egg holder bought from a kitchen equipment store. Black plastic coating really makes it stand out and also prevents rusting. The ivy variety "Mini Adam" was chosen because of the feathery appearance of the pointed, white-edged leaves.*

2 *Stuff the head with moist sphagnum moss, packing it in very tightly so that it remains in position even if it shrinks slightly. Then line the rest of the basket.*

Choose pots of ivy with long trails for quick coverage

6 ***Below:*** *Attach a handle of fine chain to the basket so that it can be hung using a butcher's hook. Adjust the position so that it hangs level.* •

3 *Fill the center with moisture-retentive potting mix such as that recommended for hanging baskets. Make sure that it is worked into the interior space properly and firm down gently.*

4 *Divide up the pots of ivy, separating out the individual cuttings. Plant them in the top of the basket, making a hole for each root clump with your fingers.*

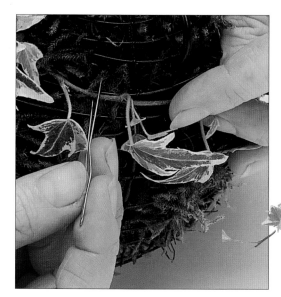

5 *Cut lengths of florist's wire into halves or thirds and bend them like hair-pins. Cover the moss-filled body with ivy by pinning the trails at intervals.*

Loose ivy trails arch down to make the tail "feathers"

A LARGE WINTER DISPLAY

The delicate combination of foliage and flower is just right for this classically-styled basket. Its pale blue-green coloring is reminiscent of ice, so we decided to pursue that theme, combining a variety of plants to give the effect of frost. We could have chosen an all-white planting, but the gradation of white through to pink is even more effective.

Ornamental cabbages and cut-leaved kales produce a central rosette of foliage which is either rich purple, pink, white, or a combination of these colors. Here a deep pink cabbage is used to highlight the much paler, frilly-leaved plant in the foreground. Ornamental cabbages tend to lose their outer leaves gradually through the winter, but the loss is usually compensated for by new growth at the center. Remove yellowing leaves with sharp scissors. Erratic watering, as well as changes in the weather, can cause the plants to bolt (flower prematurely), which looks rather odd as the center telescopes out. If this happens, replace plants with something equally bold, such as a dwarf pink-flowered bergenia like "Baby Doll."

Female varieties of the evergreen *Gaultheria* are smothered with marble-like berries by mid-fall and the fruits usually last well into late winter. An ericaceous potting mixture suits these lime-hating plants well. Hardy winter-flowering heathers such as *Erica carnea* are ideal plants for winter baskets, flowering for several months.

1 *Turn the basket upside down and, if there are no guidance marks, pinpoint the position of your drainage holes with a felt-tip pen. Drill through the plastic.*

2 *Break up polystyrene seed trays into chips to use as a lightweight substitute for gravel drainage. Fill the tapering base of this large basket up completely.*

3 *Cover the polystyrene with potting mixture. Check that the largest rootball of the plants to be used can be accommodated, allowing room at the top for watering. Lightly firm the soil.*

4 *Plant the largest element at the back of the basket and then add the pink heather.*

5 *Put the ornamental cabbages in around the opposite edge to the heather, leaving a gap in the center for the pansies. Tilt the heads slightly to show off the centers.*

6 *Fill the center with pansies— select plants with subtly different shading, dark and light, to draw all the elements of the basket together. Fill gaps with soil.*

Gaultheria mucronata
(formerly Pernettya mucronata*)*
"White Pearl"

Erica carnea "Springwood White" *(heather)*

Ornamental cabbage

7 *Water and allow to drain before attaching the three chains to the basket rim. Hang in a sunny spot, sheltered from wind. Water only when the surface of the compost begins to dry out slightly.*

Pansy—Ultima series "Pink Shades" *F1*

103

A CHEERFUL BASKET OF EVERGREENS

This bright and cheerful hanging basket will liven up even the darkest winter day.
The scarlet primroses really sparkle, and we have picked up on their bold yellow
centers by using a golden-variegated euonymus.

1 *Line the basket with black plastic and cover it with some potting mixture. This will act as a small reservoir, conserving water.*

You should find all the necessary ingredients for this basket on sale in garden centers from fall to early winter. Many young shrubs in small pots are available at this time of the year. They may seem quite expensive for use in a seasonal basket, but they really are worth it and of course they can be planted out in the garden once the display is over.

As well as the euonymus we used in this arrangement, you could also try its white-variegated counterpart "Emerald Gaiety," or evergreen herbs, and hebes such as the pink-flushed "Red Edge," or silver-leaved *Hebe pinguifolia* "Pagei."

Cineraria, though more often associated with summer bedding displays, is reasonably hardy. It is worth potting up a few plants if you have them toward the end of summer. Cut back any long straggly shoots or flower stems to promote bushy new growth and keep in a sunny spot ready for use later on.

You can always find pots of ivy with long trails in the house plant section of garden centers; those sold outdoors in winter are rarely so luxuriant. Remember to introduce the ivy to outdoor conditions and temperatures very gradually before planting.

Conifer hedge clippings make a good substitute for moss in baskets. In winter, the fresh green coloring is especially welcome— it lasts for months without turning brown. Use it thickly to help insulate the basket and prevent the soil from freezing.

2 *Using pliable leafy conifer fronds, build up a lining inside the basket, tucking the foliage under the edge of the plastic circle. Weave the pieces into each other and through the basket bars.*

3 *Plant the euonymus through the bars of the basket. Place the rootball on the potting mixture.*

4 *Continue to build up the conifer lining. Plant the silver cineraria in the top of the basket.*

5 *Plant scarlet red hybrid primroses as the centerpiece.*

Senecio cineraria "Silver Dust" (cineraria)

Hybrid primroses

Euonymus fortunei "Emerald 'n' Gold"

Hedera helix "Ester"

6 *Add a well-grown pot of trailing ivy to balance the basket design, then fill in all the gaps between the plants. Water in thoroughly.*

7 *Hang the basket in a sheltered spot outdoors, say from a hook fixed under the overhang of an open porch. Water when the compost dries out.*

EYE-CATCHING POTS OF GOLD

The life of primroses can easily be extended, especially if you chose good plants in the first place. Look for compact primroses with many buds still to come and healthy, stiff dark green leaves. Gently tip the plant out of its pot to look at the root system—this should be white in color and well developed.

Try to avoid plants which are pale and drawn looking, as these will have been kept too warm with insufficient light. Over-watering is also a common problem with primroses, causing the older leaves of the plants to yellow and rot. It is best to leave watering until the foliage has just started to go limp.

Avoid overhead watering, as this marks the foliage and flowers. Some leaves will go yellow as a matter of course and should be removed at the base with a sharp pair of nail scissors, along with any faded blooms.

Provided the basket is protected from the elements, it can be re-used time and again. After the primroses, you could continue the gold theme with dwarf daffodils or little yellow violas, and later on *Calceolaria* "Sunshine" or yellow flaming Katy (*Kalanchoe*).

1 *A simple color scheme—butter-yellow primroses and a gold chain —pick out the detailing on this delightful wicker basket.*

2 *Make the basket waterproof by lining it with plastic. Press the pleated lining into position. Trim off excess plastic to just below the rim so that it will be hidden by the soil. Black or clear plastic is most easily camouflaged.*

5 *Plant the primroses, arranging the foliage to fit around the handle and drape over the edge.*

3 *Add a layer of gravel to provide a drainage reservoir in the base to help prevent overwatering. However, do not put so much gravel in that you subsequently have difficulty accommodating the plants!*

4 *Cover the gravel with soil and then test the depth by popping in one of the primroses.*

HARDY PRIMROSES

Throughout the winter period, garden centers have tempting trays of brightly colored primroses for sale. Be careful when buying, as they are not all frost hardy—check the label or ask an assistant. Seed catalogues now offer several weather-resistant varieties, so you could grow your own supply. If you plan to grow primroses indoors, keep them in a cool, well-lit position.

6 *Fill the gaps in between plants with potting mixture, ensuring that there are no air pockets. Settle the soil in by watering, but be careful not to overwater.*

Remove yellowing leaves and faded blooms with a pair of sharp nail scissors

7 *Hang the basket in a sheltered spot. We have used an opened-out link of a larger chain as a hook.*

107

A WINTER WALL BASKET WITH BERRIES

The festive-looking winter cherry comes into the shops during late fall and makes an ideal subject for a basket by the front door over the holiday period.

1 *Cut a piece of plastic sheeting to line the back of the basket and protect the wall—one corner of an empty potting mixture bag is ideal.*

We chose pure white cyclamen, again readily available at this time of year, and white-variegated ivy as a foil for the orange-red berries. For a richer combination, you could try scarlet-red cyclamen and dark green ivy.

Although these varieties are traditionally thought of as houseplants, they will grow outside provided they have a sheltered, frost-free position—the warmth given out from the walls of a house and shelter from an overhead porch may be sufficient in areas where the winter is relatively mild or in the inner city.

4 *Guide the ivy trails through the bars, resting the rootball on top of the soil.*

2 *Line the front and sides of the basket with sphagnum moss—you can use moss salvaged from summer baskets.*

3 *Add potting mixture to fill the base of the basket to just below the level of the moss. Break up pots of rooted ivy cuttings ready for planting.*

6 *When planting the cyclamen, tilt it so that the handsome marbled foliage hangs over the edge of the basket. This also helps to prevent water from collecting in the crown and causing rotting.*

5 *Pack in more moss around the neck of each clump of ivy and continue to build the lining to the top of the basket. Plant two winter cherries toward the back of the basket, leaving a gap in the front of the basket.*

Solanum pseudocapsicum
"Thurino" (winter cherry)

Cyclamen persicum
(mini cyclamen)

Hedera helix
"Adam"
(English ivy)

❖ MAINTENANCE

The plants in this basket have slightly different watering requirements. The rootball of winter cherry should be kept constantly moist, otherwise the berries tend to drop prematurely. Ivy is quite drought-tolerant, and cyclamen should be allowed to dry out slightly between waterings to prevent rotting. Do not water overhead—use a watering can with a long, narrow spout to target more accurately.

Hedera helix
"Kolibri"
(English ivy)

7 *Fill gaps between plants with more soil and cover the surface with moss to prevent erosion when watering. Water thoroughly, allow to drain, then hang.*

109

A BASKET OF PANSIES

Wicker baskets come in all shapes and sizes. Most are unlined, but don't let that put you off planting them up—lining them is very simple. Wicker is best kept under cover to prevent it from weathering. Containers with winter bedding relish the protection of an open or enclosed porch or sunroom as they can suffer when exposed to cold winds.

Many different winter-flowering pansies are now available. The most widely sold are the weather-resistant Universal and Ultima Series. Most pansies can be made to flower through the year by sowing at different times, so do not be surprised to see summer bedding varieties on sale in winter. As plants put on little growth until spring, it is important to choose bushy specimens with healthy dark green foliage and plenty of flower buds. Avoid any which show no signs of flowering, as these are unlikely to produce blooms until the spring.

A basket edged in ivy can be planted up with all kinds of flowering plants, including hybrid primroses, double daisies, and even dwarf bulbs, provided the container is deep enough. Ignore usual spacing instructions and pack them in as tightly as possible for maximum impact. Keep in a cool but sheltered place, such as a cold frame, until the bulbs are just starting to show flower buds, then bring out onto display. If you forget to buy bulbs in the fall, garden centers have a good selection in pots for instant planting from midwinter.

Hedera helix "Mint Kolibri"

Pansy Crystal Bowl series "Sky Blue" F1

1 *Containers with a handle convert easily to hanging baskets. This wicker basket was bought ready-lined and is ideal for use indoors.*

2 *The sealed lining protects the basket but plants may become waterlogged. Add a layer of gravel to act as a drainage reservoir.*

3 *Cover the gravel with compost making sure that there is still room for the pansies and ivy on top. Check the level with a plant and adjust as necessary.*

*Add just enough water to settle
the soil around the plants. Add
more soil if gaps appear.
Thereafter, water sparingly,
allowing the soil surface to dry
out slightly between waterings*

*Pack the plants in tightly
for maximum impact*

4 *Make a continuous edging of foliage for the
basket by splitting the pots of ivy (see box).
Arrange the long trails to hang over the edges.
You could also wind some of the pieces
around the handle.*

5 *Plant the pansies in the center of the basket.
Pack them quite close together for instant
impact, as they will not grow much bigger
during the winter. Fill the spaces in between
with compost and firm in.*

6 *Use just enough water to settle compost
round the plants. Add more compost if
gaps appear. Thereafter, water sparingly,
allowing the soil surface to dry slightly.*

DIVIDING IVY

Trailing ivy is available year-round in
garden centers. It may look as though
pots contain just one plant, but closer
examination reveals seven or eight
rooted cuttings around the rim.
For our basket edging, we simply
opened out the circle of cuttings into
a straight line.

FERNS IN AN ORIENTAL BASKET

The container you select will often dictate the type of foliage and flower you choose
to plant in it. This little basket looks very similar to the pots used in Chinese
cooking, so a plant with an oriental feel was chosen to fill it.
See the panel opposite for more oriental planting ideas.

The foliage of the *Pteris* fern looks at a glance like that of dwarf bamboo and the pale biscuit color of the basket shows off the rich green fronds perfectly. *Pteris* ferns are some of the easiest to maintain and will tolerate temperatures as low as 45°F in winter. Like all ferns, they enjoy a humid atmosphere, so hang them in the bathroom or near the kitchen sink and try to remember to mist the foliage daily with tepid water. They are ideal for brightening up a north-facing window or hanging in the shaded end of a conservatory. However, keep them out of direct sunlight, otherwise the leaves may scorch.

The success of this basket demonstrates the fact that you do not need a variety of plants to make a good display. Simplicity is nearly always the key to success. If you can, try to imagine your proposed plantings in black and white so that you are able to concentrate on the form of the foliage and flower as opposed to the color. That way, you will be able to see if there is enough textural interest and overall contrast.

2 *Cover the gravel with a peat-based potting mix and try one of the ferns in for size, checking the depth, and ensuring that there is enough of a gap at the top to allow for easy watering.*

1 *Add gravel to provide a layer of drainage in the base of this ready-lined basket.*

INDOOR PLANTS WITH AN ORIENTAL FLAVOR

Red single-flowered trailing fuchsia

Clerodendrum thomsonae

Red mini-cyclamen

Foliage begonias, for example

Begonia rex hybrids

Scirpus cernuus (keep moist)

Dwarf *Cyperus* (keep moist)

Red-variegated *Coleus*

Euonymus japonicus "Aureus"

Forest cacti (*Schlumbergera* and *Rhipsalidopsis*)

Lachenalia aloides

Asparagus ferns

4 *Add remaining pteris ferns, adjusting the position so that the foliage fills the basket and works in round the handle.*

Keep plants looking their best by removing damaged fronds at the base with nail scissors

5 *Fill the gaps in between with more potting mix and firm in. Water to settle the soil.*

Pteris cretica albolineata *(variegated table fern)*

3 *Having soaked the rootballs thoroughly, put in the first plant.*

6 *Suspend the basket using natural-colored twine or raffia to blend in with the other materials used. If the basket is hung over a kitchen work surface, along with other utensils, you could also use a butcher"s hook.*

The basket is made of thin strips of wood, not bamboo, and has a wooden handle.

113

HELP!

Essential Maintenance for all Hanging Baskets **116**

Rescuing a Dried-Out Hanging Basket **118**

Deadheading and Trimming Baskets **120**

Dealing with Pests and Diseases **122**

115

ESSENTIAL MAINTENANCE FOR ALL HANGING BASKETS

Hanging baskets contain temporary, combined arrangements of plants with differing needs. Some are delicate and thus require special care and attention.

ESSENTIAL MAINTENANCE

Watering This will be your main task. In hot, dry weather, forgetting to water can spell disaster for a traditional wire basket. Regular watering which, depending on the basket size and lining, may be required up to two or three times a day at the height of summer, is essential for optimum results.

Watering tips
- If you know you will not be able to water regularly, stick to large, self-watering baskets.
- Line wire baskets with a waterproof liner.
- With moss-lined baskets, mulch the surface with a thick layer of moss and use a plastic pot saucer or large circle of plastic to act as a mini-reservoir.
- Use a planting medium containing a moisture-retaining compound.
- Hang baskets in a lightly shaded spot and avoid windy sites. Incorporate a watering funnel which directs water to the heart of the basket and helps prevent soil erosion. Water tends to roll off the surface of dry compost without penetrating. Invest in a hanging basket pulley system so that you can lower the basket easily.

- With several baskets, use a hosepipe for watering, fitting a long watering lance. A fine rose applied to your watering can or hose will shower the basket with a slow, gentle water flow, allowing water to soak in more readily. Do not rely on rain to do your watering for you!

Below: A well-cared for, properly maintained basket like this one will repay you with abundant flowers, vibrant colors and vigorous form. Regular watering, feeding, and careful protection from the weather are the keys to success.

Feeding   After about six to eight weeks, most multi-purpose composts will run out of fertilizer and you will need to begin regular liquid feeding. Alternatively, mix in a slow-release fertilizer at planting time. These are available as powder or granules or as fertilizer tabs or sticks pushed into the compost after planting.

• Select a liquid feed specifically designed for flowering plants—general purpose feeds may contain too much nitrogen, promoting leafy growth, and few flowers.

• Avoid overfeeding, which leads to lush, soft, sappy growth which is vulnerable to wind damage and insect attack.

• Feed plants regularly according to the manufacturer's instructions. If you have a tendency to forget to feed your plants, switch to fertilizer sticks or tabs, or using a dilute feed whenever you water.

• Never pour fertilizer onto dry compost—it can scorch the roots and severely damage the plant.

• Signs of starvation include slow shoot growth, with smaller than usual flowers and leaves and pale foliage, sometimes tinted red or brown. If you are already feeding regularly, consider switching to a different brand, or increasing the feeding frequency or concentration.

Checking for pests and diseases

If you check the plants over every time you water and deadhead, you should be able to deal with problems before they get out of hand. See pages 122–125 for detailed information about what to look for.

Above: *Applying a slow-release fertilizer by hand. These widely available fertilizers come in various forms and are particularly useful for those who are away from home a great deal or for people who are forgetful about feeding their plants.*

Above: *Checking a hanging basket plant for disease (in this case, an oxalis affected by rust). Plants are prone to attack from many different sources, but if you keep up the essential basic maintenance of your plants you will normally spot any problems before they become unmanageable.*

RESCUING A DRIED-OUT HANGING BASKET

Even when you are scrupulous about regular watering, in very hot weather some baskets and wall containers will dry out in no time. Here is how to fix the problem.

Above: A badly dried-out hanging basket—to be avoided at all costs! If you let your baskets get into this state, they will probably not recover.

It happens to all of us at some point! You return home to find a shrivelled basket that seems beyond rescue. Do not despair. You will be amazed at the capacity some plants have for recovery, provided you act quickly enough and follow the advice below.

Plunge the whole basket in a large container or sink of water, preferably so that the surface of the compost is submerged.

You may have to weigh the basket down to stop it floating. Wait until all the air bubbles have stopped being released and the basket feels heavy before draining.

If the compost refuses to take up water, add a few drops of liquid detergent to act as a wetting agent.

After several hours you may be lucky enough to have almost a full recovery. Busy Lizzies and brachyscome wilt alarmingly, but often spring back to life with no real harm done. If this is the case, simply trim off the odd affected shoots, and wilted flowers.

If the basket shows few signs of recovery, more drastic action may be necessary. Using sharp scissors or secateurs, trim the basket back by a third to a half of its original volume. This will take the pressure off the damaged roots, which are unable to take up sufficient water to maintain such a large quantity of foliage. Site the basket in a shady, sheltered spot out of direct sunlight and wind to further reduce water loss from the leaves. Give liquid feed with a balanced fertilizer containing trace elements to act as a tonic and to stimulate new growth. Alternatively,

Above: Soaking a hanging basket. Add detergent as a wetting agent.

Above: Leave the basket to soak for at least a few hours. Wait for obvious signs of recovery before re-hanging the basket.

Above: Brachyscome *(Swan River Daisy) is a good drought-resister with a surprising rate of recovery. Such plants are a useful staple for summer hanging baskets.*

Above: Most geraniums will fare well in bot, dry weather. This is a pink variety named "Venus."

use foliar feeds sprayed at regular intervals to assist the recovery process.

If after a couple of weeks certain plants still show no sign of regrowth, carefully dig them out of the basket and replace with fresh material. Lobelia rarely recovers, and if it is planted in the sides of the basket it can be difficult to replace late on in the season,

when the basket is full of roots. Ivy cuttings "planted" by working holes into the basket sides using a pencil may do the trick. Continue to feed and water the basket regularly until it has recovered, and then hang it back in its original position.

If you frequently experience problems with dried-out baskets due to sheer forgetfulness or a lack of time to water, consider using plants that are either drought-resistant in the first place—such as geraniums—or good "recoverers" such as those mentioned above.

Below: Geraniums are excellent plants for dry conditions. They will last well with minimal watering and recover quickly when they have wilted. Variegated Felicia amelloides *makes a good companion for such conditions, as here.*

DEADHEADING AND TRIMMING BASKETS

Nearly all cultivated plants require some assistance in order to fulfill their maximum potential. Beyond regular feeding and watering, deadheading and judicious trimming of flowers and foliage are the essential tasks. It is important to remember that a well-tended basket not only looks good, it will also go on flowering much longer.

REMOVING FADED BLOOMS

Some plants—like fibrous-rooted begonias, brachyscome and impatiens—rarely need deadheading. The same is true of plants that produce a profusion of tiny flowers, where the dead blooms tend to fade gracefully as fresh ones open. But if you do need to deadhead plants like alyssum and ageratum, use a small pair of scissors to clip off affected parts. As the plants are small and delicate, it is important to perform the operation as sensitively as possible.

Large flowers become unsightly as they fade and should be removed before seed pods develop—it is much easier to spot a fading flower amongst the foliage than a green seed pod or a developing flower bud! If you fail to remove the dead flowers, plants tend to switch their resources over to seed production and soon stop sending out as many new blooms. Nip off the dead flowers with your thumb and forefinger or, with a plant that has tough stems, use a pair of kitchen scissors. Do not leave long flower stalks uncut, especially on pansies, as these can spoil the whole display.

With some tuberous-rooted begonias that produce very large pompons, you will find a pair of insignificant looking flowers behind every one. These are the females, and they should be removed as soon as you are able to distinguish them, so that all of the plant's energies go into the central male bud, resulting in large, showy blooms.

After prolonged wet weather, peel off the shattered petals of plants like impatiens, which you will find lying saturated against

Above: *Removing faded blooms from a pansy. With most flowers just use thumb and forefinger, but tough pansy stalks should be cut at the base with nail scissors.*

120

Above: *Remove dead foliage and stems to keep the plants in your basket looking fresh. If you let dead matter accumulate, it can cause disease problems and makes the plant look untidy.*

Above: *Remove spent flowerheads from tuberous-rooted begonias to encourage the growth of new buds. Nip out the two female flower heads either side of the pompon.*

the foliage. If you do not remove them, they tend to stick on as they dry and go brown, spoiling the good looks of the basket.

Finally, do not forget to remove yellowing leaves at the same time as deadheading, to keep the basket attractive and healthy.

KEEPING A BALANCED DISPLAY

Trim back overlong trails, especially where the growth is beginning to look rather thin and straggly. Check the balance of the basket now and then and reduce the size of plants that have grown too large for their position. It is not unusual for silver *Helichrysum* and *Bidens* to get completely out of hand and swamp less vigorous types.

Above: *Pinching out a fuchsia. This technique will encourage the plant to become bushy rather than leggy, with a greater number of blooms.*

121

DEALING WITH PESTS AND DISEASES

No matter how well you prepare your hanging baskets, how carefully you tend them, and how vigorous your plants may be, there is always the risk that a pest or disease might attack the container at some point. If it happens, the important thing is to act quickly. These are the most common pests and diseases likely to afflict your plants.

Keeping your baskets and wall containers healthy is a question of good cultivation, using strong, pest- and disease-free plants to start with and taking swift action at the first sign of trouble. Here are some of the most common problems that might be encountered in your hanging garden, together with recommendations for treatment.

DISEASE PROBLEMS

Powdery mildew Powdery mildew appears like a white dust on foliage during summer,

Above: Powdery mildew on a pansy. Note the gray, weary look of the foliage. Dried-out plants are particularly susceptible.

especially when plants have been stressed by hot, dry conditions and lack of watering. Control by improving conditions. Cut out affected growth and, if necessary, use a fungicidal spray.

Botrytis or gray mold This is a fungus which mainly lives on decaying matter but which can cause problems in cold, damp conditions. It produces grayish, furry patches. Polyanthus and pansies in winter baskets are particularly susceptible. Be scrupulous about removing yellowing foliage, and dead flowers. Cut out affected growth and use a fungicidal spray if necessary.

Rust This is first noticed as yellow or orange patches on the undersides of leaves and on stems. Destroy affected plants. Control is difficult with sprays.

Virus Yellow-streaked foliage and shoot distortion point to viral infection. Control aphid and other sap-sucking insects and destroy affected plants.

Above: Gray mold (botrytis) is a problem in winter baskets and during damp conditions.

Above: *The larvae of ladybugs and hoverflies are natural predators of aphids and should be encouraged.*

PEST PROBLEMS

Aphids These are sap feeders that cause shoots to distort and shrivel up. They also introduce viruses. Try to spot aphid colonies before there is a population explosion! Look on shoot tips, flower buds, and the underside of leaves. Prolonged infestations lead to plants being covered with a sticky honeydew residue which supports the growth of black sooty mold. Leaves appear twisted and puckered, flowers few and small.

Organic control Avoid overfeeding, which causes vulnerable soft, sappy growth. Check plants regularly, nipping off affected parts with thumb and forefinger and discarding or rubbing off the aphid colonies. With a bad infestation, use a jet of water from the hose to blast off the aphids. Collect ladybugs adults and larvae and the larvae of hoverflies and transfer them to infested baskets. Sprays of soft soap solution can also be a deterrent.

Chemical control Sprays of systemic insecticide are available that reputedly do not harm beneficial insects. Spray after foraging bees have finished for the day.

Caterpillars The larvae of butterflies and moths usually feed from the edge of a leaf or flower inward, leaving a jagged margin. Some completely skeletonize the leaf and others roll them over for camouflage. Look out for the dark droppings. The size of infestation varies according to egg-laying habits, but a single large green caterpillar can do a surprising amount of damage, munching away unseen.

Below: *Caterpillars can cause a lot of damage to plants in a very short space of time. Keep a close watch on your plants for signs of butterfly or moth eggs, or caterpillar excrement.*

Organic control Do this by hand-picking or knocking the caterpillars off with a fine cane onto a piece of card. Avoid touching caterpillars that have bristles, as some cause skin irritation. A biological control spray of a bacterium that specifically infects and kills caterpillars is now available.

Chemical control Use contact insecticides for severe infestations.

Spider mites During hot, dry, summer weather these may appear on basket plants such as *Scaevola*. Barely visible to the human eye, they feed on the undersides of leaves causing yellowing, and mottling. A fine webbing may also be seen.

Organic control Predators for biological control are only effective under greenhouse conditions. Avoid siting baskets and wall containers against hot, sunny walls. In hot, dry weather maintain high humidity by frequently watering both compost and foliage.

Chemical control Systemic insecticides may be used but the pest often returns unless the physical conditions change.

Slugs and snails These creatures can be a surprise problem, having moved into the basket unnoticed before it was actually hung up! Snails can climb walls and may be found in colonies roosting behind wall planters. Both slugs and snails leave ragged holes in leaves, stems, and flowers as well as silvery slime trails, and can cause a lot of damage.

Above: *The results of red spider mite attack... The leaves of this plant are mottled and wizened and the whole impression is of unhealthiness.*

Above: *Slugs are relentless feeders which are not always easily detected. Watch out!*

Above: *Snails will climb walls to feed in planters and baskets.*

Organic control By hand picking—go out with a torch at night! Clear slugs and snails from their daytime roosting sites. Be careful where you place wall containers, as snails may lurk beneath the foliage of a climber-clad wall. Meticulously check plants before incorporating into the display. One rogue slug can do a lot of damage!

Chemical control Mainly by means of slug bait, which can vary in effectiveness.

Vine weevil

Adult vine weevils are dull, gray-brown beetles that feed at night, leaving U-shaped holes in evergreen leaves. The weevils often lay their eggs around plants grown in peat-based compost. A problem in the glasshouse and outdoors, their larvae—characteristic U-shaped, cream-colored grubs with a brown head—eat the roots of plants, leading to wilting, and sudden collapse. Vine weevils are one of the worst pests of all in containers.

Organic control By means of a microscopic nematode worm that parasitizes the grubs. Obtain it freeze-dried from biological control specialists. Collect adult vine weevils by torchlight and always check newly purchased plants for signs of infestation, removing the pot to see if the root system is well developed. If grubs are discovered, wash the soil from the roots, and re-pot. Check stored tubers before use.

Chemical control Soil insecticides are widely available and it is possible to buy pre-treated planting media to help with the problem.

Above: *Applying organic vine weevil grub control. The parasitic nematode worm* Steinernema bibionis *is sold dry to make into a solution available via garden centers. It can easily be watered onto affected plants in relatively small amounts.*

Left: *When you have exhausted all organic methods of control without success, as a last resort spray the affected plant with chemicals.... However, for the sake of your plants and the environment in general, avoid chemicals whenever you can.*

125

PLANT IDENTIFIER

A–D 128

E–I 130

L–M 132

N–S 134

S–V 136

Index 138

Acknowledgments 140

ARGYRANTHEMUM

MARGUERITE DAISY

ASTERISCUS MARITIMUS

GOLD COIN

BEGONIA SEMPERFLORENS

BEGONIA

Most of the marguerites are just too large for basket work, but the white-flowered *Argyranthemum frutescens* and *A. foeniculaceum*, which has more finely cut blue-green foliage, are suitable for larger baskets, and hay racks. Dwarf-growing, white-flowered forms are available, as well as the dainty *A.* "Petite Pink." Argyranthemums flower the whole season through and can be overwintered frost-free under glass for use the following year or propagated from cuttings taken in fall.

Best in full sun, this plant benefits greatly from deadheading, which can be carried out periodically using a small pair of hand shears, carefully shaping the plant in the process.

A relatively recent introduction to the patio plants section of your garden center, this somewhat tender perennial has a spreading habit and is useful for arching over the edge of a basket. It looks particularly effective when combined with other yellows and with dramatic foliage.

Asteriscus is a sun-loving alpine and it will not perform well in cold, exposed situations, or cold, wet summers. Grow it in a sheltered, hot spot, where its large, deep-yellow, disc-shaped flowers, and silky grayish-green foliage will stand out well. Propagate asteriscus from cuttings taken during summer and keep the rooted cuttings protected under glass over winter.

The tuberous-rooted begonias are spectacular. In *Begonia* × *tuberhybrida* growth is upright with large heart-shaped leaves and pompon blooms, but in *Begonia pendula* the branches are cascading with weeping clusters of smaller single or double flowers.

Buy tubers or plugs by mail order or from garden centers in early spring, ready to start off in a warm greenhouse. Flowers come in all shades except blues and purples. Remove the insignificant female flowers behind the central male bud for larger blooms.

The abundant and drought-tolerant *Begonia semperflorens*, fibrous-rooted begonias, come as seed-raised mixtures or single colors.

BIDENS FERULIFOLIA

BIDENS

BRACHYSCOME

SWAN RIVER DAISY

DIASCIA

DIASCIA

This tender perennial and its improved form "Golden Goddess" (available from seed), have transformed hanging baskets in recent years. They have a similar vigor to, and therefore make good partners for, the trailing Surfinia petunias and *Helichrysum petiolare* and its forms. The spreading stems, covered in small, finely-cut leaves and starry, golden-yellow blooms, make a fine cascade effect. Trim plants back periodically if they are overpowering other subjects. Happy in full sun or light shade, bidens flowers continuously right through into fall and also has a remarkable ability to recover from drought. Avoid constantly hot, dry conditions, which may lead to mildew.

Brachyscome is another relative newcomer. The scented half-hardy annual *B. iberidifolia* has undergone much improvement by plant breeders to give compact-growing mixtures and single color strains of blue, purple, pink as well as white daisy flowers. Varieties like "Purple Splendour" make striking single subject basket plants.

More commonly used in baskets, though, are the forms of *Brachyscome multifida* such as "Blue Mist." These tender perennials form low, spreading hummocks, useful for the edge and sides of baskets. Foliage is mossy and covered in a profusion of tiny daisy blooms. "Lemon Mist" is pale yellow and "Pink Mist," lilac pink.

These somewhat tender perennials are increasingly available in the patio plants section of garden centers. The unusual shell-shaped blooms open in profusion on very fine stems above a carpet of tiny leaves. Most are pink, but pale, purple-flowered cultivars such as "Lilac Belle" are also available. They prefer full sun but do not appreciate poor, dry conditions. After the first flowering in early summer, trim back the stems to encourage further flushes. The habit in a basket is semi-trailing. Pot up plants at the end of the season, trimming them back hard, and overwinter frost-free. The pink-flowered *D.* "Ruby Field" and *D. vigilis* are easy to find. "Joyce's Choice" makes long trails and "Blackthorn Apricot" is apricot-pink.

129

ERICA CARNEA

WINTER HEATHER

FELICIA

KINGFISHER DAISY

FUCHSIA

FUCHSIA

Winter-flowering heathers such as *Erica carnea* and *E.* × darleyensis make tough, long-flowering additions to baskets hung out through winter and early spring. They are normally sold as one- or two-year-old plants, but the smaller plants do not tend to flower for as long or make quite as much impact. Colors range from pinks and lilac-purples to crimson and white, and some cultivars are principally grown for their golden foliage. Trim plants back immediately after flowering. Best in full sun with moisture-retentive peaty compost.

The crimson-flowered Cape heath (*Erica gracilis*) is sold as a houseplant but will flower in a sheltered spot outdoors from late fall.

There are few sky-blue flowered bedding plants, and felicias are particularly useful for extending the color range. The daisy flowers are held on stiff stems sparsely clothed in small leaves. These drought-tolerant plants may be reluctant to flower in cool, wet summers and prefer a spot in full sun, growing alongside other heat lovers in well-drained soil. *Felicia bergeriana* is available from seed, but the more substantial *F. amelloides* is a tender perennial grown from cuttings. Try *F. a.* "Santa Anita" for larger blooms with yellow centers and "Variegata" for bright, cream-variegated foliage—eye-catching whether in flower or not.

Although quite happy in full sun, these sumptuous plants excel in cool conditions and team up nicely with busy Lizzies and begonias. There are upright bush forms as well as semi-pendulous and trailing types, which are excellent for baskets. Varieties sold in garden centers tend to be the tried and tested standards such as "Swingtime," "La Campanella," "Dollar Princess," "Jack Shahan," and "Marinka." Flower form ranges from elegant singles to full doubles with "skirts," like crinolines. Two-tone blooms are common and colors range from white and palest pink through to crimson and magenta, and many shades of purple. Variegated and gold-leaf cultivars are also available. Easy from cuttings.

HEDERA HELIX

ENGLISH IVY

HELICHRYSUM

HELICHRYSUM

IMPATIENS

BUSY LIZZIE

You will find scores of varieties including "Adam," "Eva," "Kolibri," and "Sagittifolia," but plants are rarely named. The lobed evergreen leaves are plain green or edged and marbled with varying amounts of white or yellow. The greater the variegation, the less hardy the cultivar. Plants are sold as individual rooted cuttings or in pots with several cuttings, which are easy to split up to use singly. Ivy is indispensable for fall, winter, and spring baskets, and you can recycle plants from summer baskets which have grown long trails. Ivy is happy in shade and quite drought tolerant, but watch for red spider mite in hot, dry conditions.

The silver-gray leaved *Helichrysum petiolare* is a classic basket plant with stiff, spreading branches covered in round, felted leaves. It rarely suffers from pests or diseases, is sun-loving and drought tolerant. The only drawback is that it can swamp less vigorous basket plants, so cut back periodically through the summer to maintain balance. *Plechostachys sepyllifolia*, formerly *H. microphyllum* is a daintier substitute with tiny leaves. Unlike some lime-green leaved foliage plants, *H. p.* "Limelight" is happy in full sun and useful for adding sparkle to contemporary color schemes. The pretty "Variegata" has cream and gray-green variegated leaves and is less vigorous.

This well-known bedding plant comes in a myriad shades, excluding yellow, and blue. Petals may be plain or edged with a darker margin as in picotee types, or variously striped and blotched. There are subtle pastel mixtures as well as vivid assortments of red, pink, and orange. For consistency of performance, go for F1 hybrids including individual color selections from the "Accent," "Novette," and "Super Elfin" series. Large-flowered hybrids include the vivid orange "Tango," and "Blitz Violet". Busy Lizzies are a mainstay of shady baskets but will grow in full sun, though deep colored flowers may bleach. Keep thoroughly well fed and watered.

LAMIUM MACULATUM

DEAD NETTLE

LOBELIA

LOBELIA

LOBULARIA MARITIMA

SWEET ALYSSUM

A creeping ground-cover plant, the variegated dead nettle has in recent years crossed over to baskets. Available as little pots or plugs of rooted cuttings, plants soon cover the basket sides. Leaves have a central stripe of silver or are virtually covered in silvery white. Hooded flowers appear on more established plants in shades of white, clear pink, mauve, or cerise. Two of the most striking for baskets are "White Nancy," and "Pink Pewter." "Roseum" is also widely available and you can find golden yellow forms including "Aureum." Lamiums thrive in shade and dislike hot dry conditions, which can lead to powdery mildew.

Lobelia erinus varieties are split into bush and trailing types *L. e. pendula*. The latter are particularly useful for basket work producing a frothy mass of tiny flowers to complement larger blooms of plants like petunia and begonia. For a blend of blues, pinks, purples, and white try the "Cascade" or "Fountain" mixtures, or go for single color selections like the pretty "Lilac Cascade." "Sapphire" is deep blue with a white eye. You will also come across the tender perennial *L. richardsonii*, with pale blue flowers on wiry trails. Excelling in shade, lobelia requires constantly moist compost and recovers poorly from missed waterings.

Much more commonly known as sweet alyssum because of its powerful honey fragrance, this bedding plant has undergone a transformation in recent years with the development of pink and purple shades, and pretty pastel mixtures including peachy tints. Being a hardy annual, alyssum is quick to set seed and stop flowering, especially if under stress through lack of water. But, breeders have produced several more reliable kinds, notably the pure white "Snow Crystals," to give a continuous summer show. It is tricky to deadhead alyssum individually because the flowers are so tiny, so instead trim them back periodically using a pair of scissors.

LOTUS BERTHELOTII

PARROT'S BEAK

This tender perennial produces long feathery trails of silvery-blue tinted foliage. Later in the season, but only in long, hot summers, exotic claw-like blooms in deep red or orange appear scattered down the length of the stem. If you are using lotus as a foliage plant in a pastel arrangement, just nip off the flowers to maintain the scheme. Lotus needs full sun to bring out the best coloring of its needle-like leaves and is reasonably drought tolerant, so it is an ideal plant for baskets hung against a hot wall. Try it with orange and flame-red sun lovers, such as geraniums, portulacas, nasturtiums, and marigolds.

LYSIMACHIA NUMMULARIA

CREEPING JENNY

A ground-hugging perennial carpeter, creeping Jenny will also produce long trails in hanging baskets. It is mainly used as a foliage plant with stems clothed in pairs of small, rounded leaves but buttercup-like blooms appear in early summer. "Aurea" is less vigorous with bright, lime green trails—excellent for shade. Stems root at each node, so it is easy to produce lots of cuttings. *Lysimachia congestiflora* is a tender perennial with shorter trails but much more showy, deep-yellow flowers borne in clusters throughout summer. Try varieties like "Lysii," "Golden Falls," and the gold-variegated "Outback Sunset." Grow in sun or shade but keep moist.

MIMULUS

MONKEY FLOWER

The monkey flower ought to be more popular as a bedding plant. With its unusual blooms featuring heavy speckling at the throat, it adds an exotic touch to plantings. *Mimulus hybridus* used to be available only in citrus mixtures of yellow and orange, but now pastel shades have arrived on the scene, widening the scope for color combinations. F1 hybrids are available in single colors or mixtures with the compact-growing "Calypso" and "Malibu" most widely available. The monkey flower is excellent in shade along with busy Lizzies, begonias, pansies, and lobelias, but like these others, it must have moist conditions. Deadhead regularly to maintain flowering.

NEMESIA CAERULEA

NEMESIA

PELARGONIUM

GERANIUM

PETUNIA

PETUNIA

Unlike *Nemesia strumosa*, the common multi-colored bedding plant raised from seed in spring, forms of this tender perennial from South Africa have smaller flowers in profusion and give a continuous show throughout the season. Bedding nemesias tend to stop flowering unless they are regularly deadheaded, especially during dry spells, but these perennials have far greater staying power and better drought resistance, forming bushy upright plants. Like diascias, cultivars of *N. caerulea* are relatively new to the patio plant scene, but each year the choice gradually broadens. Colors are all in the soft pastel range, giving a pretty and elegant effect in baskets and containers. Look out for "Elliot's Variety," "Joan Wilder," and "Woodcote."

All pelargoniums thrive on poor, dry soil, and though they prefer full sun, do surprisingly well in dry shade. Geraniums now come in many shades including pastels and bicolors, with single or fully double flowers.

The introduction of the trailing or ivy-leaved geraniums from continental Europe (Balcony, Mini-cascade) brought superior flower power to baskets. These have long trails smothered in red, pink, lilac, or white blooms. Other trailers include showy cultivars such as "Lilac Gem," "Amethyst," and the prettily variegated "L'Elégante."

The upright Zonal pelargoniums have a darker banding on their large, rounded leaves. Some are brightly variegated and a few have lime-green leaves. Try Century and Video series.

Trailing or bushy and compact petunias have single or double blooms and some are sweetly scented—smaller, single flowers perform better in wet summers. There is an extremely wide range of colors—some with darker veining and some striped or edged in white. Trailing types are now dominated by the Surfinia series (available as plants only). You can also try individual colors of the trailing "Wave Series," from seed.

Compact, free-flowering kinds with many small flowers include the milliflora or junior petunia types, for example "Fantasy" F1 hybrid series and the really tiny-flowered "Million Bells" and "Carillon" series. The larger multiflora petunias include the net-veined "Plum Pudding" and "Mirage" series, and plain "Carpet" series.

PORTULACA GRANDIFLORA

PORTULUCA

PRIMULA

PRIMROSE/POLYANTHUS

SCAEVOLA AEMULA

SCAEVOLA

If you have a hot, dry spot and are looking for a bright, cheerful basket plant, consider portulaca, a half-hardy summer-flowering annual. They should be more widely grown, as they now come in quite a wide range of colors from vivid reds, pinks, oranges, and yellows to soft pastel pinks, lilac, apricot, and white. Most have single, buttercup-shaped blooms, but there are also more showy semi-doubles. These succulent, drought-tolerant plants have semi-trailing stems clothed in narrow fleshy leaves. Varieties include "Calypso" F2, "Sundance," "Cloudbeater," "Peppermint" (striped petals), and "Sundial." Flowers tend to close when the sun goes off them and they may rot off if they are overwatered.

Hardy primroses and polyanthus team up with winter-flowering pansies to make colorful winter and spring baskets. During the coldest winter months, they perform best given some shelter and maximum sunshine to encourage flower production. Go over plants regularly, removing yellowing leaves and faded blooms to lessen the risk of gray mold. Take care not to allow baskets to get too dry. Try the hardy, early-flowering primroses like the jewel-colored Primula "Wanda Hybrids," and "Husky". Polyanthus are hybrids between cowslips and primroses with intermediate flower structure consisting of a short central stem topped with blooms. Try the popular "Crescendo" series, which is available as single color strains.

A relative newcomer, this tender perennial is rather like a giant lobelia. The stiff semi-trailing stems bear toothed leaves and clusters of soft lavender-blue, fan-shaped blooms with a refined, elegant appearance. Scaevola looks best in a mixed hanging basket with frothy fillers like trailing verbena and the contrasting blooms of plants such as petunia, which help camouflage the slightly straggly stems. Scaevola has better drought resistance than lobelia, but in hot, dry conditions can suffer from red spider mite. Plants are not always named, but you are most likely to come across "Blue Fan" (correctly named "Blue Wonder"). Propagation is done from cuttings.

SENECIO CINERARIA

CINERARIA

This plant, formerly named *Cineraria maritima*, is a widely grown foliage bedding plant which is often discarded at the end of the summer season. However, it is quite hardy and evergreen and the silvery-white, felted leaves make a wonderful addition to winter baskets. Though principally grown for its attractive, lacy-cut leaves, larger specimens in semi-permanent arrangements may produce branching flower stems with insignificant yellow daisy flowers. Cut plants back at this stage to keep them compact. Senecio is exceptionally drought tolerant, and like the geranium will thrive in poor conditions. The most common forms are "Silver Dust," and the less finely cut version, "Cirrus."

SUTERA CORDATA

SUTERA

Formerly known as *Bacopa*, this is a relative newcomer with a cascading habit, making it highly suitable for baskets. The stems are much branched and densely clothed in very small leaves—a variety with golden foliage has recently become available. Tiny starry flowers stud the foliage mound all summer long, provided plants are fed and watered regularly; they tend to suffer with repeated droughts. Usually the white form "Snowflake" is grown, but there is also a pretty lilac-mauve called "Lilac Pearls" for pastel schemes. Currently plants are only available as rooted cuttings, either by mail order or from the garden center.

TAGETES

FRENCH MARIGOLD

Tagetes make mounds of finely cut foliage, in the Gem series studded with small orange, gold, or lemon-yellow blooms. Newer kinds, including "Paprika," with deep-red blooms edged in gold, and the maroon "Ornament," have broadened the choice. "Starfire" is a popular mixture. Plants rarely need deadheading and do well with full sun and good drainage. Avoid overfeeding. French marigolds are more upright, with coarser foliage available in a similar range of colors with single, double, or crested blooms. Varieties are numerous including the "Boy o' Boy" series, "Naughty Marietta," and "Tiger Eyes." Deadhead to keep plants tidy and flowering well.

TROPAEOLUM MAJUS

NASTURTIUM

VERBENA

VERBENA

VIOLA

PANSY OR VIOLA

The nasturtiums are best planted as part of a mixed basket. Their large, rounded leaves and spurred blooms provide an excellent contrast in form. The so-called climbing nasturtiums have the longest trails, but more compact forms like the "Whirlybird" series are often better in baskets, producing flowers more freely. Overfeeding causes lush leaf growth at the expense of flowers, but "Alaska," with its white marbled leaves, is a useful addition regardless of whether or not it is in flower. For handsome foliage and flowers, try "Empress of India," which has dark-red blooms and deep-bronze leaves. Watch out for caterpillar damage.

These are available as either bushy, upright plants grown from seed or as semi-trailing types raised from cuttings. A wide range of colors is available, excluding yellow and orange, with many vivid, jewel-like shades as well as pastels like the "Romance" series and the soft apricot "Peaches and Cream." The foliage of the trailers is deeply cut and fern-like, with domed flower clusters at the shoot tips. Good choices for baskets are' the vigorous "Homestead Purple," pale pink "Silver Anne," deep pink "Sissinghurst," and members of the "Tapien" series. Stems may need cutting back to keep baskets in balance. Avoid hot, dry conditions that can lead to mildew.

Pansies and violas are best grown in moisture-retentive compost and do well in light shade. At the garden center, you will find plants in bloom year round, depending on when they were sown. Certain strains perform well in winter, such as the weather resistant "Universal" and "Ultima" series, available as single colors and mixtures. Soft-shaded mixtures are very much in vogue, for example, "Antique Shades" and "Water Colors Mixed." The smaller-flowered viola mixtures include "Sorbet," "Bambini," and "Cuty," and the "Miniola Heart" series. Pansies and violas benefit greatly from deadheading, taking care to remove the flower stems. Fungal diseases may be a problem in cold, damp weather.

137

INDEX

This index lists all the projects, styling methods, and techniques mentioned in this book.
It also comprises entries for essential tools, materials, and important ancillary information.
For a general guide to the book, see the list of contents on page 9.

A, B

Alpines 23
A–Z of hanging basket plants 128–137
Backdrop for a basket 40–1
Basket of pansies 110–11
Baskets, where and how to hang 34–5
Bedding/patio plants 20
Bolt 102 (see also flowering prematurely)
Bracket, fixing to a wall, how to 35
Buckets full of bulbs 50–1
Bulbs, dwarf varieties 50
Butcher's hooks 15

C

Campanulas in silver baskets 54–5
Cascade of white and gold 88–9
Character wall pot with ivy hair 62–3
Cheerful basket of evergreens 104–5

Choosing container plants 78
Choosing your plants 20–5
Classic white arrangement 80–1
Color Guide 26–31
Colors
    cool 40
    hot 40
    schemes (see also Color Guide) 49, 82
Compost, types of 17
    coir 17
    peat 17
    recycled 17
    soil-less 17
Cottage garden basket 58–9
Culture Virus Indexed (CVI) 79

D

Dahlias in a wicker basket 96–7
Deadheading and trimming 120–1
    keeping a balanced

display 121
    pinching out 121
Difficult conditions 32
Dividing ivy 111
Drainage 48, 50, 66, 102

E

Ericaceous potting mixture 102
Essential maintenance for hanging baskets 116
Establishing a hanging basket 32–3
Evergreen shrubs 23

F

F1 hybrids 20, 131, 133–4
F2 hybrids 20–1, 135
Feeding and watering 33, 36–7
    fertilizer sticks/tabs 18
    foliar feed 33
    overfeeding, effects of 117
    feeding, tips 117

Ferns in an oriental basket 112–13
Fitting a large plant into a basket, how to 95
Flowering prematurely 102 (see also bolt)
Fragrant jasmine in a black wire basket 56–7

G

Geraniums in a wirework wall basket 68–9
Grass and succulents in a terracotta wall pot 86–7
Growing under glass 32–3

H, I

Half-hardy annuals 20
Hanging baskets for a hot sunny spot 84–5
Hanging baskets for a shady place 72–3
Hanging baskets, types of 14–15
    flower towers 15

hanging pockets 15
hay racks 15
mangers 15
novelty 15
plastic 14
self-watering 14
wall 14
wicker 14
wire 14
Hardening off 32
Hardy primroses 107
Healthy plants, what to look for 21
Herbaceous perennials 23
Herbs 23
Hostas in a woodland basket 72–3
Houseplants 23
Hyacinths and primulas 48–9
Ivy chicken basket 100–1

L

Large display of purple and yellow 90–1
Large winter display 102–3
Late-season pastel display 94–5
Lime-hating plants 102
Liners and composts 16–17
coir/coconut fibre 16
conifer clippings 16, 104
felt/recycled wool 17
plastic sheeting 17
sphagnum moss 16
sponge 17
Liquid fertilizer 18, 36

M

Mail order, buying by 24
Making an impact with baskets 42–3
Making plants fit the available space 84
Making the most of hanging baskets 10–11

N, O

Nitrogen 36
Oriental-style plants 113
Overwintering 83
asparagus ferns 83
begonias 83

P

Perennials 20
Pests and diseases 117, 122
aphids 123
botrytis or gray mold 122
caterpillars 123
chemical controls 123–5
organic controls 123–5
powdery mildew 122
rust 117, 122
slugs and snails 124
spider mites 124
vine weevil 125
Pink basket for cool shade 74–5
Plant identifier 126–37
Planting up for summer 64–5
Plants, how to choose 20

Plugs (*see also* tots and rooted cuttings) 18, 20, 64
Polystyrene chips 102
Positioning baskets 43
Pots of gold 106–7
Preparing your basket 18–19
Pricking out 20

R

Rescuing a dried out hanging basket 118
Romantic hanging basket 82–3
Rooted cuttings (*see also* plugs) 18

S

Self-watering capillary matting 46
Self-watering spring basket 46–7
Shallow basket 66–7
Silver baskets of Campanulas 54–5
Slow-release pellets or tablets 36
Slow-release fertilizer granules/powder 17, 19
Spring wall basket 52–3
Starter kits 21
Styling hanging baskets 26
Subtropical hanging basket 92–3
Summer basket with a purple theme 70–1

Summer display in a manger basket 78–9

T

Terracotta wall pot 86–7
Thyme, sage and verbena 76–7
Tots (*see also* plugs) 64
Trailing plants 89
Trugs 66

V, W

Vacation care 38–9
capillary wick, how to make a 38
Violas and ivy with a fuchsia for foliage 98–9
Wall basket of portulucas 84–5
Watering 36
attachments 36
dried out basket, how to revive 37, 118
funnel 18
mini reservoir, how to make a 36
self-watering baskets 36
tips 116
Weathered look, painting pots for a 60–1
Weather-resistant pansies 110
Winter wall basket with berries 108–9
Wirework basket 68–9

ACKNOWLEDGMENTS

The majority of the photographs featured in this book have been taken by Neil Sutherland and are © Salamander Books Limited. The publishers wish to thank the following photographers for providing additional photographs, credited here by page number and position on the page, i.e. (B) Bottom, (T) Top, (C) Center, (BL) Bottom left, etc.

Elm House Nursery: 27(BR), 29(CL), 30(BL), 130(TR)
Garden Picture Library: 23(B), 24(L), 29(BL), 128(TL), 130(TL), 131(TL, TC), 133(TL, TC), 135(TL), 136(TC)
John Glover: 12, 14(T), 34(L, R), 35(TL, BL), 40(T, B), 41(L, R), 42(L, R), 43(TL, TR, BR)
Peter McHoy: 14(BL, TR), 15(TL, TR, BC), 17(TR, BR,), 18(T, B), 19(T, B), 32(L, R), 33(TL, TR, B), 116(B), 117(T, B), 118(TL, TR, BR), 119(BR), 120, 121(TL, TR, BR), 122(L, R), 123(L, R), 124(T,BL, BR), 125(T, B)
Clive Nichols: 25
S.E.Marshall & Co.:22(TR)
Suttons: 24(R), 30(BR), 137(TC)
Thompson & Morgan: 10(R), 20(L, R), 27(BL, C), 28 (TR), 126, 134TC, TR), 135(TR), 137(TR, TL)
Unwins Seeds Ltd: 21(B, T), 23(T), 26(L, R), 28(BL), 29(BR), 31(TL, B), 119(BL), 128(TC), 129(TC), 131(TR), 132(TC), 133(TR), 134(TL), 135(TC), 136(TL)

The publishers would like to thank Grosvenor Garden Center, Belgrave, Chester, England and Bridgemere Garden World, Nantwich, Cheshire, England for supplying plants and containers for photography.